1000 FACTS ON
MAMMALS

First published by Bardfield Press in 2005
Copyright © 2002 Miles Kelly Publishing Ltd

Bardfield Press is an imprint of
Miles Kelly Publishing Ltd,
Bardfield Centre, Great Bardfield, Essex, CM7 4SL

Some material in this book first appeared in the *1000 Things You Should Know* series

2 4 6 8 10 9 7 5 3

Editor
Ruth Boardman

Design
White Design

Indexer
Jane Parker

Picture Researchers
Liberty Newton, Bethany Walker

Repro
profile imaging

British Library Cataloguing-in-Publication Data
A catalogue record for this book is available from the British Library

ISBN 1-84236-148-1

Printed in China

www.mileskelly.net
info@mileskelly.net

1000 FACTS ON
MAMMALS

Duncan Brewer

Consultant: Steve Parker

BARDFIELD
PRESS

Contents

Key

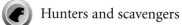
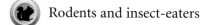
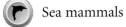

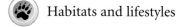

Contents

Contents

Contents

Tigers

- **At over 3 m long** and weighing up to 360 kg, the rare Siberian tiger is the largest living member of the cat family. Tigers originated in Siberia.

- **Tigers need a very large hunting area**, and males in northern India often patrol an area of 130 sq km or more.

- **After feeding**, tigers sometimes save the remains of a kill for a later meal, burying it under branches to hide it from scavengers or other tigers.

- **In 1945 there were only 50 Siberian tigers** left in the wild; now there are 300 to 400 surviving in reserves.

- **Aggressive tigers** flash the distinctive white spots on their ears as a warning.

- **In India and Bangaladesh**, in the Sunderbans mangrove swamps, tigers keep cool in the water and ambush pigs, deer and monkeys.

- **In the early 1900s** there were probably at least 50,000 tigers; now numbers have fallen to 6000 or less, half of them living in India.

▼ *To keep out the cold, the Siberian tiger has an outer coat of long, pale fur over a thick undercoat.*

▲ *The tiger uses its long canine teeth to bite the throat or neck of its prey as it brings it to the ground. Its sharp-edged rear teeth cut through the meat by sliding against each other like scissors.*

- **A tiger's stripes camouflage it** as it hunts in the tall grasses by day. But tigers also hunt at night – their night vision is at least 6 times more acute than a human's.

- **Tiger cubs** depend entirely on their mothers for food until they are about 18 months old, when they begin to make their own first kills.

...FASCINATING FACT...
Tigers eat a variety of foods, ranging from fish and turtles during times of flood to locusts during locust swarms.

Wild dogs

- **The South American bush dog** pursues prey into the water, and, unlike most dogs, can swim underwater.

- **African Cape hunting dogs** live in packs in which only the dominant female has young.

- **Cape hunting dog cubs** are left in the den, protected by adult guardians, while the pack hunts, and are fed with disgorged meat when it returns.

- **Cape hunting dogs** do not creep up on prey, but approach a herd openly, selecting a single target to chase.

▼ *Cape hunting dogs are well camouflaged; no two individuals have the same markings.*

- **Cape hunting dogs** can run at 60 km/h for 5 km or more. They may travel 50 km a day while hunting, and patrol a range of 1500 to 2000 sq km.

- **Indian wild dogs**, or dholes, hunt in packs of up to 30, and can drive tigers and leopards from their kills.

- **Dholes** hunt in thick undergrowth, advancing in an extended line until they have flushed out their prey.

- **The raccoon dog** of east Asia eats insects, shellfish and fruit.

- **Australian dingoes** are probably descended from Indian wolves that were domesticated in Asia and taken by Aboriginal settlers to Australia, where they reverted to the wild.

◀ *Dingos and domestic dogs have bred with each other for so long that there are only a few pure bred dingoes.*

. . . **FASCINATING FACT** . . .
Cape hunting dog females may fight over possession of their puppies, often killing them.

11

Thylacine or Tasmanian wolf

- **The Tasmanian wolf**, or thylacine, was a meat-eating Australian marsupial that probably became extinct when the last known one died in captivity in 1936.

- **Once common throughout Australia** and New Guinea, the Tasmanian wolf retreated to Tasmania some 3000 years ago, driven out by dingoes.

- **The Tasmanian wolf** had a pouch that opened to the rear, where the young spent their first 3 months.

- **Also called the Tasmanian tiger**, because of its stripes, the Tasmanian wolf was in fact neither a wolf nor a tiger.

- **Like a kangaroo**, the Tasmanian wolf had a thick-based tail and would hop on its back legs if chased.

- **The jaws of the Tasmanian wolf** opened almost 180°, allowing it to kill an animal by crushing its skull.

- **With its immensely powerful jaws**, the Tasmanian wolf could kill a pursuing hunting dog with one bite.

- **Fossil remains** of an animal almost identical to the Tasmanian wolf were discovered in America.

- **Tasmanian wolves may survive** in the dense forest, but this remains to be proved.

▶ *Some people claim to have seen Tasmanian wolves still surviving in remote parts of Tasmania.*

···· **FASCINATING FACT** ····
Thousands of Tasmanian wolves were killed in the late 1800s, because they preyed on sheep.

Cheetahs

▲ *The cheetah's tail helps with balance during high-speed sprints.*

- **Unlike most cats**, cheetahs can hardly retract their claws at all. The claws grip the ground as they run, like the spikes on a sprinter's shoes.

- **A cheetah** can accelerate from 0 to 72 km/h in 2 seconds, and can reach a top speed of 120 km/h.

- **A silver vase** (c.2300 BC), found in the Caucasus, shows a cheetah in a collar, which suggests people used cheetahs then as hunting animals.

- **The 16th-century Mogul emperor** Akbar kept 1000 cheetahs, which he used to hunt blackbuck.

- **Cheetahs** have the same body length as leopards, but stand a good 35 cm taller on their long legs.

- **In the Kalahari Desert**, cheetahs can survive for 10 days without water by eating wild melons.

- **Young male cheetahs** often hunt in small groups (coalitions), and are healthier than solitary males.

- **A cheetah** will chase a warthog that runs, but will usually leave one that stands its ground.

- **If a cheetah does not catch its prey** in the first 300 to 400 m of the chase, it gives up and allows its heart beat to return to normal.

- **Cheetahs** avoid lions, which will kill them.

▼ *Cheetahs often sit on rocks or termite mounds to get a better all-round view when resting.*

Otters

◀ Otters are naturally playful creatures and are most active at night.

- **Otters** enjoy playing games, such as dropping pebbles into water and catching them on their heads!

- **The African clawless otter** can move its thumb across the other fingers to hold onto objects.

- **Clawless otters** gather tough-shelled freshwater mussels with their hands, and take them ashore to smash them on rocks.

- **When hunted by hounds**, otters have been known to drag their pursuers under water and drown them.

- **Otters** have special whiskers on their muzzles and elbows that are sensitive to water disturbances and help them to locate prey.

- **Giant otters** clear a series of 7 m wide areas around their territories before scent-marking them.

- **The male Eurasian otter** patrols a territory of up to 50 km of riverbank; the female's territory is about 10 km.

- **The marine otter** of the west coast of South America is the smallest sea mammal in the world, weighing no more than 4.5 kg.

- **Some otters**, including the Cape clawless otter and the Oriental short-clawed otter, catch their prey in their paws rather than in their mouths.

◀ *The otter's coat is made up of a dense layer of underfur, with an outer layer of long guard hairs.*

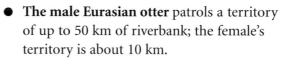

...FASCINATING FACT...
The giant otter of Brazil is the longest of the otter family, at almost 2 m long .

Badgers

◀ *Different generations of badgers use the same burrow system, called a sett. Each family might make their own alterations or add more tunnels.*

- **Successive generations of Eurasian badgers** use the same den or sett, sometimes for over a century.

- **The ferret badger** is the smallest member of the badger family, and the only badger to climb trees.

- **The honey badger** is led to bee nests by the greater honey-guide bird, which attracts it with special calls, and feeds on beeswax once the badger has opened the nest.

- **The desert-dwelling American badger** can burrow fast enough to catch a ground squirrel burrowing in the ground ahead of it trying to escape.

- **A female Eurasian badger** sometimes has female helpers that baby-sit her cubs, often in their own nests, while she forages for food.

- **Despite a bear-like appearance**, badgers belong to the mammal group known as mustelids, and are related to otters and weasels.

- **The honey badger's extremely tough skin** protects it from all kinds of dangers, ranging from bee stings and porcupine quills to snake bites.

- **Badgers** are enthusiastic housekeepers – they regularly change their bedding, and also dig latrines some distance from their setts.

- **Earthworms** are one of the badger's favourite foods, and females suckling their young feed on little else.

- **Eurasian badgers** will enlarge their favourite setts. One ancient den consisted of 879 m of tunnels, with 178 entrances and 50 subterranean chambers.

▶ *The skin of the honey badger (also known as a ratel) is so loose that the animal can twist right round and bite the attacker who has a grip of it by the scruff.*

19

Hedgehogs

- **The Eurasian hedgehog** has between 5000 and 7000 spines on its back and sides, each erected by its own muscle, creating a defence difficult for predators to penetrate.

- **When a hedgehog rolls into a ball** at the approach of danger, a special muscle draws its loose skin together (like a drawstring on a bag) over its head and rump.

- **From Roman** to medieval times in Europe, it was believed that hedgehogs often carried a supply of fruit with them, impaled on their spines.

- **Over 150,000 hedgehogs** are killed every year on the roads of France alone.

- **The moonrats** of Southeast Asia and China are closely related to hedgehogs, but have no spines.

- **The long-eared** and desert hedgehogs of Asia and North Africa dig their own individual, short burrows.

- **Hedgehogs** can go without water for long periods, and if dehydrated will drink half their bodyweight in one go.

▶ *Scent is important to hedgehogs, as they communicate and track food by smell.*

◄ *The hedgehog gets its name from its piglike habit of foraging in hedgerows searching for food.*

- **A western European male hedgehog** has a foraging territory of up to 35 hectares.

- **Lack of food** rather than cooling temperatures causes a hedgehog to hibernate.

...**FASCINATING FACT**...
The hedgehog keeps up a ceaseless whistling sound while hunting for food.

Domestic dogs

- **All modern domestic dogs**, from chihuahuas to Great Danes, are direct descendants of grey wolves.

- **Grey wolves** were first domesticated over 12,000 years ago in Europe and Asia, for use as guards and herders.

- **Female domestic dogs** can have two litters of puppies a year; wild members of the dog family have only one.

- **The Portuguese water dog** can be trained to dive and retrieve fishing equipment in fresh or salt water.

- **Bloodhounds** can pick up a trail over two weeks old, and follow it for over 200 km.

- **The caffeine compounds** in a bar of dark chocolate can kill a dog weighing up to 5 kg.

▼ *The chihuahua is a tiny smooth haired domesticated dog which originated in Mexico.*

- **St Bernard** rescue dogs work in teams of three – two to keep the victim warm, one to fetch their handler.
- **Some dogs** can sense when their owner is about to have an epileptic fit, and others can detect skin cancers before the recognized symptoms appear.
- **During World War II**, over 50,000 dogs were enlisted in the US forces, performing tasks from sentry duty to stealing enemy documents.
- **Native Americans** used dogs to drag a type of sledge.

▼ *Male St Bernard dogs often weigh over 90 kg.*

Polar bears

◄ Apart from pregnant females, which spend the winter in dens where they give birth, polar bears are active all through the winter months, often travelling great distances in search of food.

● **The polar bear** is the only bear which is almost exclusively a meat-eater, other bears eat plants too.

● **While stalking a seal**, a polar bear will sometimes lie on its chest with its front legs trailing at its sides and its rump in the air, pushing itself forward with its rear legs.

● **Polar bears** can detect the scent of seal pups in dens buried 1 m deep in snow.

● **Lying in ambush** for a seal, a polar bear will sometimes cover its black nose with its paws to remain unseen against the snow and ice.

● **Polar bears** have a number of tiny protrusions and suction pads on the soles of their feet to give them a firm grip on the ice.

● **The most southerly place** that polar bears regularly visit is James Bay in Canada, which is on the same line of latitude as London.

● **Female polar bears** can put on as much as 400 kg in weight in the course of their summer feeding binge on seal cubs.

- **The polar bear** is a powerful swimmer, even though it uses only its front paws as paddles, letting its rear legs trail behind.

- **Beneath its thick white fur**, a polar bear's skin is black. Translucent hairs channel heat from the sun to the animal's skin, which absorbs the heat.

▼ *Outside the breeding season, polar bears are normally solitary animals.*

...FASCINATING FACT...
Female polar bears may go without eating for up to 8 months – existing solely on their body fat – while overwintering and feeding their newly born young.

Grizzly bears

- **The great hump** behind a grizzly's head is solid muscle, enabling it to overturn 50-kg rocks with its front paws, or kill an elk with a single blow.

- **During its winter sleep** the grizzly loses about 1 kg of bodyweight each day. Some grizzlies emerge from their sleep 50% lighter.

- **Grizzlies** once ranged across the USA, with numbers as high as 50,000–100,000; but as their terrain has been taken over by humans, their numbers have fallen to 6000–8000.

- **Most grizzlies are dark brown** in colour, but regional colouring ranges from black to very pale yellow.

- **Despite their great size**, grizzlies are nimble enough to catch squirrels and mice, and can reach a speed of over 55 km/h when charging.

- **Native Americans** had great respect for the grizzly, and apologized before killing it, sometimes laying out ceremonial clothes for it to wear in the spirit world.

▶ Alaskan grizzlies feed heavily on migrating salmon.

◀ Grizzly mothers give birth to their cubs in their dens in winter, and go on to look after them for anything up to a further 4-5 years. During these early years their mothers teach them to forage and hunt and protect them from predators.

- **Grizzlies** are immensely strong. They have been known to bite through cast iron, bend rifle barrels, and open up cars like sardine cans in search of food.

- **Originating in China**, the ancestors of the modern grizzly crossed land bridges from Asia to North America some 40,000 years ago.

- **Grizzlies** often enter their winter dens just ahead of a snowstorm, so that the snow covers up their fresh tracks and seals them in for their long winter sleep.

...**FASCINATING FACT**...
The huge Kodiak grizzly bear of the Alaskan coastal islands can reach a height of 3 m on its hind legs, and weigh up to 1 tonne.

27

The weasel family

- **In years of vole plagues**, the European common weasel may have up to three litters, because food is available.

- **Pest control** of American prairie dogs has led to the extinction of the black-footed ferret in much of its range.

- **Tribesmen** in Burma are reported to have used trained weasels to kill wild geese and the young of wild goats.

- **The 25 kg wolverine**, the largest weasel close relative, has large feet for hunting reindeer in deep snow.

- **Male weasels** are often twice the size of females, and eat different prey, reducing food competition.

- **Bred for the fur trade**, many American mink escaped into the European countryside, replacing European mink and depleting water vole populations.

- **Ferrets**, traditionally used in Europe to catch rabbits, are a domesticated form of the European polecat.

- **Black-footed ferret young** are cared for by their mother in a separate burrow until they are self-sufficient.

- **In New Zealand**, introduced weasels have almost wiped out some native birds by eating their eggs.

▲ *This least weasel is most active after dark, but will hunt in the daytime.*

▼ *A mink's broad diet includes fish, bringing it into direct competition with otters.*

···FASCINATING FACT···
The American least weasel, at 15 cm long and weighing 30 g, is the world's smallest carnivore.

Leopards and jaguars

- **A leopard can carry** a prey animal three times its own weight up a tree, out of reach of scavengers.

- **Black panthers** are leopards with black pigmentation. Any leopard litter may include a black cub.

- **The South American jaguar** is America's only big cat.

- **A frozen leopard carcase** was found on Mount Kilimanjaro, Africa, at an altitude of 5692 m.

- **The jaguar catches** not only fish, but also otters, turtles, alligators and frogs.

- **Snow leopards**, which inhabit the mountains of Central Asia, have never been known to roar.

- **The snow leopard** has paws cushioned with hair to act as snow shoes. In the Himalayas it seldom goes below 2000 m, and sometimes goes as high as 5500 m.

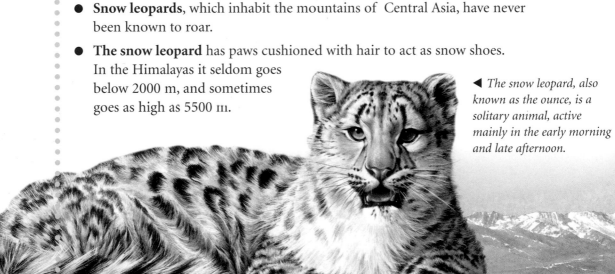

◀ *The snow leopard, also known as the ounce, is a solitary animal, active mainly in the early morning and late afternoon.*

- **Leopards** have survived successfully partly because they will eat almost anything, from crabs to baboons.

- **By far the best** climber of the big cats, the leopard sometimes drops straight out of a tree onto its victim.

- **The jaguar** was worshipped as a god by early South American cultures.

▲ *The leopard is by far the best climber of the big cats, and often sleeps in the branches, as well as storing food there.*

31

Lions

- **The largest-known wild lion** was an African male man-eater, shot in 1936, and weighing 313 kg (the average male lion weighs 150–190 kg).

- **Male lions** have the job of protecting the pride, leaving the hunting to the females most of the time. But the males insist on eating first from any kills!

- **Lions** are the only big cats that lead social lives, hunting together and sharing their prey.

▶ Only male lions have a mane, which shows off their size, and also protects them during fights. The females are the main hunters in the pride.

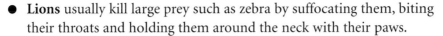

- **Lions** usually kill large prey such as zebra by suffocating them, biting their throats and holding them around the neck with their paws.

- **When a foreign male** takes over a pride of lions by driving off its leading male, he kills cubs under about 6 months old and mates with their mothers.

- **Lions** spend most of their time sleeping, usually dozing for about 20 hours of the day.

- **Once widespread** throughout Southwest Asia and India, the only lions now surviving outside Africa are a few Asiatic lions in the Indian Gir Forest wildlife reserve.

- **Buffaloes and elephants** are a particular threat to lion cubs, and will go out of their way to kill them.

- **A male lion** will not usually allow other pride members to share a kill until he has had enough.

> **...FASCINATING FACT...**
> A male lion can eat up to 30 kg of meat at one sitting, and then will not need to eat again for several days.

33

Mongooses, civets, genets

- **African banded mongooses** gang up together to repel and attack predators such as jackals.

- **The Malaysian binturong** is related to civets, and is the only Old World mammal with a prehensile tail, which it uses as a brake when descending trees.

- **The palm civet** of Asia is known as the toddy cat, because it has a taste for a fermented alcoholic drink.

- **Civets** were once kept captive in Ethiopia and 'milked' of their strong-smelling musk, which was used in the perfume industry.

- **A mongoose** will tire out a cobra by making quick movements, then kill it.

- **The dwarf mongoose** marks its territory by doing a handstand to deposit a scent mark as high as possible on a rock or bush.

- **Common genets** are found in France and Spain. They may have been introduced in medieval times as pets and rat-catchers, by the Moors of North Africa.

- **Otter civets**, like true otters, have webbed feet and closable nostrils. They catch fish and can climb trees.

- **Largest** of the civet-mongoose family, the fossa of Madagascar has a cat-like head and retractable claws.

- **In fights** against members of the same species, some mongooses curl over and present their posterior to their opponent, biting at him between their hindlegs.

Small-spotted genet

African genet

Malayan civet

▲ *Many civets and genets hunt for food in trees as well as on the ground.*

Mountain lion or puma

- **The mountain lion**, or puma, is the widest-ranging American mammal, occurring from Canada in the north to southern Chile in the south.

- **Mountain lions** are the largest American desert carnivores.

- **The Patagonian** puma has a hunting territory of up to 100 sq km. Its main prey is the llama-like guanaco.

- **As a form of territorial marking**, pumas build little piles of soil or vegetation called scrapes.

- **In the Sierra Nevada**, the main prey of mountain lions is the mule deer, which can be twice the lion's weight.

- **High altitude** varieties of mountain lion may be much larger (113 kg) than those living lower down (45 kg).

- **Below the timber line**, the mountain lion hunts by night. At higher altitudes it may have to hunt by day.

- **There are few reports of mountain lion attacks** on humans, but attacks have increased as humans have taken over more of the mountain lion's territories.

- **Mountain lions** are solitary, avoiding one another except to mate. When the young leave their mother, they relocate at least 45 km away.

▼ *Baby big cats are called cubs. Puma cubs have spotty coats when they are first born. These fade as they get older.*

FASCINATING FACT
Although the size of a leopard, the mountain lion is classified as a small cat because it can purr.

Black bears

- **American black bears** vary in colour from black, through brown, cinnamon, honey and ice-grey, to white, according to regional races.

- **Beavers** are a favourite food of some black bears, because of their high fat content.

- **In autumn**, feeding up for the winter sleep, black bears put on up to 1.5 kg per day.

- **Black bears** mate in the summer, but the fertilized egg does not begin to develop until the autumn, and the cubs are born in January or February.

▼ *Black bears occasionally raid people's beehives and orchards, as well as city dumps.*

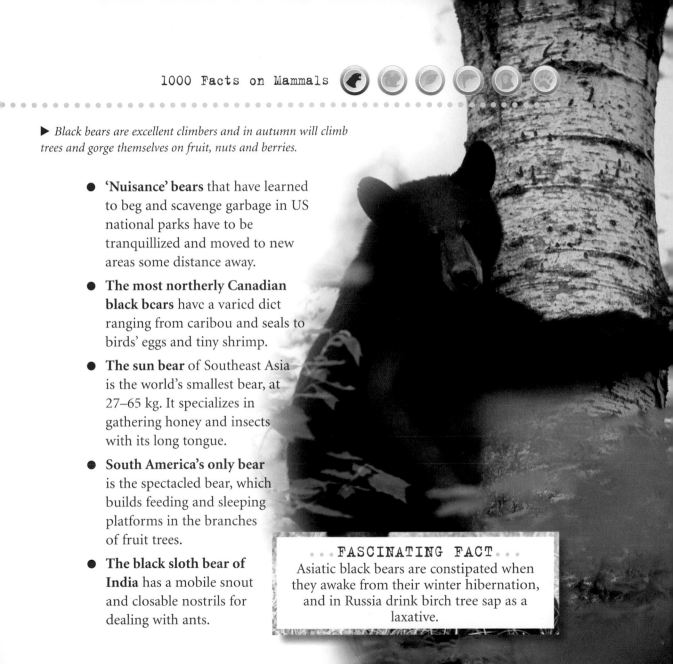

▶ *Black bears are excellent climbers and in autumn will climb trees and gorge themselves on fruit, nuts and berries.*

- **'Nuisance' bears** that have learned to beg and scavenge garbage in US national parks have to be tranquillized and moved to new areas some distance away.

- **The most northerly Canadian black bears** have a varied diet ranging from caribou and seals to birds' eggs and tiny shrimp.

- **The sun bear** of Southeast Asia is the world's smallest bear, at 27–65 kg. It specializes in gathering honey and insects with its long tongue.

- **South America's only bear** is the spectacled bear, which builds feeding and sleeping platforms in the branches of fruit trees.

- **The black sloth bear of India** has a mobile snout and closable nostrils for dealing with ants.

... **FASCINATING FACT** ...
Asiatic black bears are constipated when they awake from their winter hibernation, and in Russia drink birch tree sap as a laxative.

Lynxes and bobcats

- **Bobcats and lynxes** are closely related, but the lynx inhabits northern conifer forests and swamps, and the bobcat prefers rocky regions with dense undergrowth.

- **Lynxes have shorter tails** than bobcats, and their longer legs help them to move through deep snow.

- **Chased by dogs**, the bobcat often takes to water, where it is a superior swimmer to its pursuers.

- **In experiments**, bobcats with clipped ear-tufts heard less well, suggesting the tufts aid their hearing.

- **Lynxes have thick fur** on the soles of their feet to keep them warm and help prevent slipping on icy surfaces.

▶ *Bobcats are normally solitary animals, sleeping throughout the day and hunting at night. Though ground dwelling, this cat will climb trees and take to water when chased.*

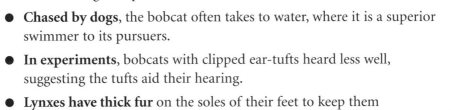

. . . FASCINATING FACT . . .
Snow hares provide 70% of the North American lynx's diet. Lynx numbers fluctuate with the 10-year population cycle of the snow hare.

▶ *Long ear tufts help the lynx to hear its main prey, the snow hare, and long legs enable it to chase its prey through deep snow.*

- **The bobcat is only found in America**, but the lynx has populations across Europe and Asia.

- **Bobcat kittens** are taught to hunt by the age of 7 months. At 12 months the mother drives them away.

- **Unlike the lynx**, the bobcat flourishes in deserts.

- **The bobcat may live up to 20 years**, eating rabbits, prairie dogs, rattlesnakes and crayfish.

Wolves

- **In wolf packs**, only the dominant female normally mates and has cubs. The female wolves sometimes fight to establish who is to be the pack mother.

- **Forest wolves** stay all year in their own territory, while tundra wolves are nomadic, following the migrations of prey such as caribou.

- **Wolves howl** to avoid territorial fights – if they know where another pack is, they usually steer clear of it.

- **Grey wolves** often go for a week without food. They only average one kill in every 10 hunting expeditions.

- **Although they normally hunt large prey** such as deer, wolves will also eat carrion, berries and even fish.

- **Wolf packs** may number 20 or so where moose are plentiful, but only 6 or 7 where deer are the main prey.

▶ *The grey wolf is the ancestor of the domestic dog, and still occasionally mates with dogs such as huskies.*

- **Tundra wolves** hunt larger prey than wolves further south, and tend to be larger themselves.

- **A pack's dominant pair** scent mark the home range (up to 1000 sq km) by urinating about every 3 minutes.

- **Wolves migrated** into Europe, Asia and Africa from North America some 7 million years ago.

- **Wolves cull** the old and weak members in a herd of prey animals, improving the herd's overall health.

▲ *The grey wolf has a strong muscular body with a thick coat, which ranges in colour from almost white in the Arctic to nearly black in the south.*

43

Raccoons

◄ *Raccoon young, born in the spring start to go out with their mother at about 2 months old. They stay with her until the autumn.*

- **In many suburban areas of the USA**, raccoons have moved into sheds and roof spaces, emerging at night to raid garbage cans.

- **Hunting raccoons** with 'coon dogs at night is popular in the southern states of the USA, but raccoons have been known to lure dogs into water and then drown them.

- **Raccoons** use their slender-fingered front paws to capture frogs and crayfish.

- **Raccoons** have a weakness for sweet corn, raiding crops just ahead of the farmer.

- **The crab-eating raccoon** of South America leads a semi-aquatic life, and is also a good tree climber.

- **Raccoons** belong to a family that includes long-tailed kinkajous, coatis and cacomistles in the Americas, and the red pandas in Asia.

- **In the northern part of their range,** raccoons may retire to their nests in winter for a month or two.

- **Captive raccoons** appear to wash food before eating it, but in the wild a raccoon's underwater manipulations are to locate food rather than to wash it.

- **In urban areas,** raccoons sometimes carry off garbage cans, even untying rope knots to remove lids.

▼ *The raccoon's distinctive 'mask' fits its reputation as a night-time bandit, thief and garbage raider.*

···FASCINATING FACT···
At one time raccoon skins were used as currency in parts of Tennessee, USA.

45

Hyenas

- **After making a successful kill**, the spotted ('laughing') hyena emits a blood-curdling, laugh-like cry.

- **The aardwolf** is a small, insect-eating member of the hyena family. One specimen was found to have over 40,000 termites in its stomach.

- **Often portrayed as a skulking scavenger**, the spotted hyena is in fact an aggressive hunter, and is also capable of driving lions from their kills at times.

- **The hyena's powerful jaws** can crush large bones, which its digestive system dissolves in a few hours.

- **Hyenas** may suckle their young for more than 1 year, compared to 2 months in the dog family.

▶ *The hyenas' victim is often brought down by a bite to the leg or back and then ripped to pieces by the pack while it is still alive.*

◄ *A spotted hyena can chase a wildebeest for 5 km at a speed of 60 km/h.*

- **All hyenas hide surplus food** for later – sometimes even underwater in the case of the spotted hyena.

- **Hyenas** are more closely related to mongooses than to members of the dog family.

- **In South Africa**, brown hyenas, or 'beach wolves', beachcomb for dead crabs, fish and sea mammals.

- **A female brown hyena** was once seen to take a springbok carcase from a leopard, and drive the leopard up a tree.

- **Brown and striped hyenas** erect their long manes to make them look larger when displaying aggression.

Coyotes and jackals

- **Silver-backed jackals** lived in Africa's Olduvai Gorge some 1.7 million years ago, and still live in the region.

- **The coyote** is probably the only predator whose range is increasing across North America.

- **Coyotes can live to be over 14 years old** in the wild, and over 21 years old in captivity.

▲ *Male and female jackals are similar in appearance though the male tends to be slightly larger.*

- **Jackals are fearless defenders** of their family groups – a single jackal will attack a hyena five times its weight.

- **Farmers who poison coyotes** to reduce attacks on their livestock may be increasing the numbers of attacks, by killing the coyote's natural prey.

- **Native Americans** celebrated the cunning 'trickster' coyote, and told myths about its cleverness.

- **The golden jackal** of Eurasia and Africa is fond of fruit, eating figs, berries, grapes and desert dates, as well as animal prey.

- **When fighting** a predator or stealing a kill, pairs of jackals employ a 'yo-yo' technique, dashing in from each side alternately.

- **Without a 'helper'**, an average of one silver-backed jackal pup survives each litter, but with a helper three survive, and with three helpers an average of six survive.

▼ *A keen hunter, the coyote's prey ranges from mice to sheep.*

FASCINATING FACT

Young coyotes may spend a year helping to
raise their younger brothers and sisters.

The smaller cats

- The **fishing cat** of Southeast Asia and India inhabits marshes and swamps, and has slightly webbed paws. It preys on fish, birds and small mammals.

- The **Iriomote cat** is probably the world's rarest cat. Less than 100 exist, on a remote, mountainous island off southern Japan.

- The **black-footed cat** of South Africa is the smallest wild cat. It spends the day in disused burrows, and eats spiders and beetles as well as small rodents.

- The **serval** is a cat of tall grasses, with very long legs and neck. It locates prey with its prominent ears, catching it with a high, fox-like pounce.

- The secretive **Andean mountain cat** lives at altitudes of up to 5000 m, protected from the cold by its fine fur and long, bushy tail.

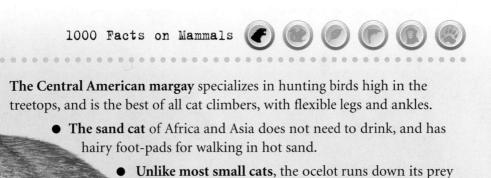

- **The Central American margay** specializes in hunting birds high in the treetops, and is the best of all cat climbers, with flexible legs and ankles.

- **The sand cat** of Africa and Asia does not need to drink, and has hairy foot-pads for walking in hot sand.

- **Unlike most small cats**, the ocelot runs down its prey instead of ambushing it, and is an excellent swimmer.

- **The smaller cats purr**, but cannot roar.

◀ *The long-legged caracal eats rats, hares, birds, and baby animals such as antelopes and wild pigs. It also eats lizards and snakes.*

> **... FASCINATING FACT ...**
> The caracal is a lynx-like African cat weighing
> up to 20 kg. It can kill antelopes twice
> its own weight.

51

Domestic cats

- **Domestic cats** probably evolved from African wild cats, which were domesticated as early as 4000 BC in Egypt.

- **The ancient Egyptians revered cats**, and believed they held the daylight in their eyes.

- **Clay tiles** in a Roman temple in Britain bear the imprint of cats' paws. It is likely that the Romans introduced domestic cats to the British Isles.

- **The long-haired Turkish Van cat** is sometimes called the swimming cat, and is known in Turkey for attending lakeside picnics, playing in the shallows.

- **Some 98% of the patched cats** known as tortoiseshells, or calico cats, are females.

▼ *Domestic cats have retained their wild hunting instincts, and are major predators of garden birds.*

- **The Maine Coon**, the oldest breed of domestic cat in the USA, may have Viking origins.

- **In 1950 a 4-month old kitten** followed some climbers to the summit of the Matterhorn in the Swiss Alps.

- **Siamese cats** were once found only in Thailand's temples and palaces. One king's favourite cat was entombed with him, but it later escaped.

- **In November 1939**, in Devon, a tabby cat called Puss celebrated its 36th birthday, and died the following day.

- **In the 10th-century**, a kitten was worth 2 pence before it caught its first mouse, and 4 pence afterwards.

▲ *The white variety of the Persian breed of cats, can be found with three different eye colours: orange, blue and odd (one orange and one blue).*

53

Skunks

- **The skunk squirts a sticky spray** at its enemy from glands under its tail. It can reach a target up to 6 m away, and is accurate up to 2 m.

- **The skunk's spray**, which consists of 7 different chemical components, can cause temporary blindness.

- **Before spraying**, a skunk warns its enemy by stamping its feet. The spotted skunk does a handstand and walks with its hind legs in the air.

- **Skunks** belong to the same family as weasels and polecats, all of which have smelly sprays, but the skunk's spray is the smelliest of all.

- **Vets** recommend that dogs which have been sprayed by a skunk should be given a bath in tomato juice.

- **Most predators avoid skunks**, but it is a favourite prey of the great horned owl, which has a poor sense of smell and catches it at night!

- **Skunks have little fear of humans** and are often sold as pets – after a de-scenting operation.

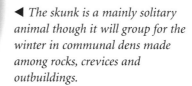

◀ *The skunk is a mainly solitary animal though it will group for the winter in communal dens made among rocks, crevices and outbuildings.*

- **Skunks are great diggers**. They use their long, straight claws to rip apart rotten logs for grubs, and to dig in sand and mud for turtle eggs.

- **Skunks sleep in communal dens** when temperatures reach freezing, with up to 20 skunks in a den.

····**FASCINATING FACT**····
In the USA, skunks are major carriers
of rabies.

▼ *Skunks eat mainly live prey, such as insects and small mammals, and also enjoy fruit and birds' eggs.*

Meercats

▲ *Meerkats live in groups of up to 30 individuals in a complex warren system.*

- **Young meerkats** care for their younger brothers and sisters while their mother forages for food to maintain her milk supply.

- **Grey meerkats** often share their burrow systems with ground squirrels.

- **If surprised in open ground** by a hawk, the adults in a meerkat pack will cover the young with their bodies.

- **The grey meerkat** attacks intruders without warning or threats, and kills with an energetic shaking, followed by a neck bite.

- **Meerkats** enthusiastically attack and eat scorpions, first rendering them harmless by biting off their tail stings.

- **Meerkats warm themselves up** in the morning sun, standing tall on their hind feet and tails, while constantly on the lookout for enemies.

- **Meerkats dig** for many food items, such as beetles, moth pupae, termites and spiders.

- **Living in the arid regions** of South Africa, the meerkat sometimes obtains moisture by chewing Tsama melons and digging up plant roots.

- **Faced with attack**, the normally slim meerkat becomes almost spherical, its hair bristling, tail up and back arched as it growls, spits and rocks to and fro.

▶ *Meerkats often act as guards on the lookout for predators. Standing on rocks or in bushes they cluck and cheep warnings to the other members of the pack.*

...FASCINATING FACT...
Meerkat warrens can cover an area of up to
25 m by 32 m, with 90 separate entrances.

57

Foxes

- **The larder of one Arctic fox** was found to contain 50 lemmings and 40 little auks, all lined up with tails pointing the same way and their heads bitten off.

- **African bat-eared foxes** have huge ears for radiating heat away from the body.

- **Arctic foxes** live only 480 km from the North Pole.

- **The grey fox** of North and Central America is the oldest surviving member of the dog family, first appearing up to 9 million years ago.

▲ *Fox cubs stay with their parents for up to a year, and will often go out with their mothers foraging for food.*

- **The African fennec fox's** 15-cm long ears are the largest of any carnivore.

- **The American grey fox** leaps with ease between tree branches.

- **Some foxes roll about** and chase their tails to 'charm' rabbits, which seem fascinated and come closer, allowing the fox to make a grab.

- **The red fox** has adapted with great success to urban life, even moving into houses via cat flaps.

- **When locating insects** beneath the ground, the bat-eared fox cups its large ears, gradually pinpointing the exact position of the prey before digging.

- **In early autumn**, up to 90% of the red fox's diet may consist of apples, blackberries and other fruits.

▲ *Basically a night hunter, the red fox is often seen during the day, and shows up sharply against winter snow.*

Porcupines

◄ *A porcupine's quills are soft when it is born, but harden within a few hours.*

- **When threatened,** some African porcupines erect their detachable quills and run backwards at their enemy.

- **African crested porcupines** warn off would-be predators by vigorously shaking their tail quills, producing a sound like the rattle of a rattlesnake.

- **The North American porcupine** has very poor eyesight.

- **Crested porcupines** are the longest lived of all rodents, the record being over 27 years.

- **American porcupines** are particularly vulnerable to attacks by fisher martens, which turn them over onto their backs to kill them, thus avoiding the quills.

- **The prehensile-tailed porcupines** of South America are active at night, and move to a new tree every 24 hours.

- **Baby porcupines** are born with soft quills to make the birth easier. Within a few hours the quills harden.

- **Some North American porcupines** have a craving for salt, and have been known to gnaw gloves, boots and saddles that are salty with sweat.

- **Old World porcupines** are not tree-climbers.

▶ *The North American porcupine will spend most of its time climbing trees and feeding on the flowers, nuts, shoots and berries.*

. . . FASCINATING FACT . . .
Some porcupines collect bones, which they gnaw on to sharpen their teeth. The bones provide them with phosphate.

Beavers

- **Beavers** are born with innate dam-building instincts. In zoos, they regularly 'repair' concrete dams with twigs.

- **It takes two adult beavers** about 15 minutes to gnaw their way through a tree-trunk with a 10 cm diameter.

- **Mother beavers** push tired youngsters ahead of them through the water, like swimming floats.

- **Storing extra oxygen** in its lungs and body tissues, a beaver can remain under water for up to 15 minutes.

- **Beavers use the split claws** on their hind feet for grooming and spreading waterproof oil.

- **A beaver signals danger** by smacking the water with its tail. The noise carries over 1 km.

▼ *The secretion glands in the base of this Eurasian beavers tail produce an oily waterproofing substance that is spread through the coat when grooming.*

- **The territory-marking secretion** of the beaver contains the main ingredient in aspirin.

- **Beavers' dams** and lodges can help create environments for fish.

- **In some parts of the USA,** beavers are parachute-dropped into areas where remote rivers need damming to reduce erosion.

▲ *The beaver uses its huge incisor teeth to gnaw through branches and tree trunks.*

...**FASCINATING FACT**...
European beavers took to living in burrows to avoid hunters. They are now protected by law.

Aardvarks

- **When in danger,** the aardvark can dig at great speed, and can outpace a team of men armed with spades.

- **An aardvark** has several burrows on its territory, often many kilometres apart.

- **Termites and ants** form the main food of the aardvark, which digs through concrete-hard termite mounds to reach them.

- **To stop termites and dust** entering its nose, the aardvark has stiff bristles on its muzzle, and can close its nostrils.

- **A moderate blow to the head** can kill an aardvark, which depends on its acute senses and digging abilities for survival.

- **If attacked** before it has time to burrow, the aardvark may roll onto its back and lash out with all four feet at once.

- **The aardvark swallows** its food without chewing, grinding it up in its stomach using special muscles.

◀ The aardvark usually feeds at night, eating termites in the wet season and ants in the dry season.

> **FASCINATING FACT**
> 'Aardvark' is Afrikaans for 'earth-pig' (but in fact aardvarks do not belong to the pig family).

- **Baby aardvarks** depend on their mothers for about 6 months, when they learn to dig burrows.

- **Some African peoples** who also eat termites keep an aardvark claw as a charm to increase the harvest.

◄ Termites make amazing mound nests. The tallest mounds can measure up to 9 m in height, which the aardvark will smash using its powerul forelimbs.

65

Squirrels

- **Grey squirrels** have been known to kill and eat rabbits, rats, cockerels and stoats.

- **Flying squirrels** are nocturnal, and when gliding may emit high-pitched squeaks that help them to locate a landing place.

- **North American red squirrels** tap birch and maple trees for their sweet sap in spring.

- **Many squirrel species** spread woodland trees by burying nuts and then forgetting where they put them.

- **The North American red squirrel**, or chicaree, buries green pine cones in damp soil to delay their ripening until they are needed.

- **The largest member of the squirrel family** is the alpine marmot, at 73 cm long not including the tail.

  - **Southeast Asian giant squirrels** prefer to hang upside down by their hind feet while eating.

    - **Chipmunks**, or ground squirrels, store huge quantities of nuts in a single cache.

      - **To prevent it slipping backwards** down a tree trunk, the scaly-tailed flying squirrel presses the horny scales of its tail against the trunk.

      - **An adult red squirrel** can sniff out a pine cone buried 30 cm deep.

▲ *The chipmunk is one of the most common small mammals in North America.*

▼ *The squirrel's bushy tail is a good balancing aid and rudder when climbing and leaping.*

Rats

- **New World wood rats,** or pack rats, continually gather twigs and build them into mounds near their nests.

- **Polynesian voyagers** carried rats on their boats as a form of live meat.

- **One species of the Southeast Asian** bandicoot rat has a body and tail length of almost 1 m!

- **To stop the black rat** stowing away on ships, mooring ropes are sometimes fitted with metal cones, which the rats cannot get past.

- **Baby Norwegian rats** signal to playmates that their play-fights are not serious by occasionally flipping over onto their backs.

- **Rats** constantly investigate their environment, which makes them good problem-solvers in laboratories.

- **Observers have seen** old, experienced rats deliberately kick traps around until they are sprung, before taking and eating the bait in safety.

- **Norwegian or brown** rats are natural burrowers, and expert at colonizing human buildings.

- **Following heavy rains** in drought regions, 19th-century Australian settlers were subjected to plagues of long-haired rats that devoured anything at ground level.

▼ *The black rat is also called the house rat, roof rat and ship rat.*

▲ *Rats are among the world's most successful mammals. This desert pack rat has large ears to enable him to detect danger from a distance*

· · · FASCINATING FACT · · ·
The black rat was indirectly responsible, via its fleas, for the death of 25% of the entire human population of Europe by bubonic plague between 1347 and 1352.

Bats

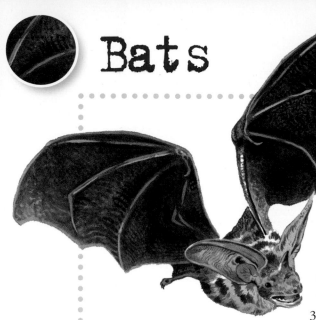

◀ *Bats are the only true flying mammals.*

● **The earliest insect-eating bat fossil** is 50 million years old, and the earliest fruit bat fossil only 35 million years old, so they probably evolved from different ancestors.

● **The bumblebee bat** of Thailand is the world's smallest mammal. Its body is just 3 cm long, and it weighs only 2 g.

● **In one North American cave**, 10 million Mexican free-tailed bats give birth each year to 10 million young over a period of about a week.

● **Bat species** form 22% of all the world's mammals, and are by far the most common rainforest mammal.

● **In some bat species**, males are known sometimes to produce milk, but it is not known if they ever suckle the young.

● **A resting bat** emits 10 sound pulses per second, rising to 30 per second as it flies, 60 per second when approaching an object, and 200 per second when approaching an insect.

> **. . . FASCINATING FACT . . .**
> The vampire bat uses razor-sharp teeth to make tiny cuts in the limbs of sleeping mammals, and then laps up the blood.

- **Australia's ghost bat** is the continent's only meat-eating bat. It hunts and devours frogs, birds, lizards, small mammals, and even other bats.

- **The bulldog bat** feeds on fish, grabbing them from the surface of the water with its specially elongated toes.

- **Many tropical nectar- and pollen-eating bats** are important pollinators of plants, including some trees. They transfer the pollen from one plant to another as they feed inside the flowers.

▶ *Bats produce high-pitched sounds that cannot be heard by humans or other animals. The sound waves bounce off the food they hunt, such as insects, then back to the bat, telling the bat where the food is.*

Anteaters

- **To protect their long, curved digging claws**, giant anteaters have to walk awkwardly on the knuckles of their front feet.

- **Anteaters have no teeth.** They use their extremely long, sticky tongues to gather up termites after breaking into their concrete-hard mounds.

- **The tamandua and pygmy anteaters** of South and Central America use their prehensile tails to climb trees, in search of termite and ant nests.

- **The Australian numbat** is the only marsupial adapted to feed exclusively on ants and termites. It has a long, sticky tongue but short, weak claws.

- **Giant anteaters**, over 2 m long from nose to tail tip, cover themselves with their bushy tails when sleeping.

- **Baby anteaters** ride clinging to their mother's backs until they are half her size.

▼ *The giant anteater sleeps up to 15 hours a day, and has one of the lowest mammal body temperatures at 32.7°C.*

- **Even jaguars are deterred** by the sharp, slashing claws of a giant anteater reared up on its hind legs.

- **The 15-cm long pygmy anteater** has jointed soles to its feet that help it to climb the trees in which it lives.

- **The mouth** of the giant anteater is so small that you could not insert a finger into it.

- **Fossils** found in Germany show that anteaters lived there over 50 million years ago.

◀ The anteater's tongue is covered with tiny backward pointing spines and sticky saliva, to which its tiny prey adhere.

73

Moles and shrews

- **Shrews** have to forage and eat almost continuously, day and night, to avoid dying of starvation.

- **The Namib golden mole** 'swims' through the desert sand, using its hypersensitive hearing to locate its insect prey.

- **The pygmy white-toothed shrew**, weighing about 2 g, is the smallest living land-based mammal on the planet.

- **European desmans** are aquatic members of the mole family, with long, flat tails, waterproof fur and webbed toes.

- **The African armoured shrew** has such strong vertebrae that it can survive being stood on by a full-grown man.

- **After their milk teeth have gone**, shrews usually only have one set of teeth. When these wear out, the shrews die.

- **Some European water shrews** have stiff hairs on their feet and tail that trap air bubbles, enabling them to scurry across

▲ *Most of a mole's food comes from the creatures that fall into its tunnels.*

the surface of water.

- **Baby shrews** may follow their mother in a line, each one holding a mouthful of the rump of the one in front.

- **The star-nosed mole** has 22 mobile, pink tentacles around the end of its snout, which help it locate prey underground.

- **The American short-tailed shrew** has enough venom in its bite to kill 200 mice.

▶ *The shrew's eyes are tiny and of little use. It relies totally on its keen sense of smell and hearing.*

75

Lemurs

- **All lemurs** live on the island of Madagascar, where they evolved in isolation, separated from the African mainland by the 300 km wide Mozambique Channel.

- **In lemur groups** the females are the more aggressive protectors of territory than the males.

- **Early European travellers** to Madagascar described a giant lemur, now extinct, that was as large as a calf.

- **Contesting male lemurs** transfer scent from their wrist glands onto their tails, then use their tails to hurl scent 'bombs' over their heads at their rivals.

- **Lemurs were able to evolve** into their many species on Madagascar mainly because they had no competition from monkeys or other primates.

- **Long after Madagascar broke away** from Africa 65–50 million years ago, the lemurs' ancestors crossed the slowly widening channel on rafts of floating vegetation.

▶ *The ring-tailed lemur uses its distinctive tail to signal to others of its species. It may live in groups of up to 30 individuals.*

Aye-aye

Coquerel's mouse lemur

- **The aye-aye**, a close relative of the lemurs, has huge ears and can hear grubs chewing wood beneath bark. It extracts them with an elongated middle finger.

- **The indri** is the largest lemur, at up to 1 m from its nose tip to its almost tail-less rump.

- **Fat-tailed dwarf lemurs** sleep through the dry season in July and August, living on the fat stored in the thick bases of their tails.

- **Lemurs groom** using a special claw on one finger, and their front teeth, which resemble a comb.

▲ *The aye-aye has an elongated middle finger which he uses to pick grubs from under the bark of trees.*

77

Capybaras and coypus

▲ *The capybara spends much of its life in the water, and has webbed feet.*

- **The South American capybara** is the world's largest rodent, a water-loving giant up to 134 cm long and 64 kg in weight.

- **Capybaras graze** in large groups on river banks. At the first sign of danger they dash into the water and the adults surround the babies.

- **South American coypu females** suckle their young while swimming, from rows of teats high on their sides.

- **Coypu** were hunted almost to extinction in the 1800s for their thick, soft fur, overlain with coarse hairs.

- **Captive farming of coypu** for what was called 'nutria' fur began in the 1920s. Many countries now have feral populations established by escaped captives.

- **The male capybara** has a hairless scent gland on its snout called the morillo (Spanish for 'small hill').

- **Capybaras mate in the water**, but give birth on land. All the females in a group feed the young if they have milk.

- **Catholic priests** once allowed capybaras to be eaten during Lent, because they considered them to be close relatives of fish (which were permitted to be eaten).

- **A capybara can stay under water** for up to 5 minutes, sleeping there with only its nose sticking out.

- **Some extinct capybara** weighed as much as a grizzly.

▼ *The eyes, nostrils and ears of the capybara are set on the top of its head to enable it to see, smell and hear while swimming.*

Armadillos and pangolins

- **The South American three-banded armadillo** can roll itself up into an impenetrable ball.

- **For swimming across rivers**, some armadillos increase their buoyancy by inflating their intestines with air.

- **The giant armadillo** has up to 100 small teeth.

- **The African giant pangolin** has a long tongue that extends internally as far as its pelvis.

- **The 9-banded armadillo** has four identical, same-sex young per litter, all developed from one egg.

> ▼ *The leathery skin and the bony armour on the 9-banded armadillo account for more than one sixth of its total weight.*

... FASCINATING FACT ...
Stone Age people used the 1.5 m high shell of the Glyptodon, an armadillo, as a shelter.

9-banded armaddillo

Naked banded armaddilo

Pink fairy armadillo

- **The armadillo's armour** is made up of small bone plates covered in heavy skin; the pangolin's consists of overlapping plates of horn.

- **The long-tailed tree pangolin** and the white-bellied tree pangolin hardly ever leave the trees.

- **Pangolins** often use only their back legs when running.

- **The long-tailed tree pangolin** has 37–46 tail vertebrae – a mammal record for the most tail bones.

▼ *Armadillos walk mainly on their hind legs, with their forelegs just brushing the ground.*

Giant armadillo

3 banded armadillo

Hair armadillo

6-banded armadillo

81

Voles and lemmings

- **At up to 2 kg**, the American muskrat is 130 times heavier than most voles.

- **Every 3 or 4 years** some vole and lemming species undergo population explosions, followed by high numbers of deaths from stress and food shortages.

- **The mole-lemming** of the Central Asian steppes digs tunnels using its protruding incisor teeth.

- **Eurasian water voles** live in river bank burrows with entrances below the level of the water's surface.

▼ *The lemming builds its nest under the snow in winter. The nest is made on the ground from dry plants and twigs. The lemming makes tunnels under the snow from its nest to find grass, berries and lichen to eat. During the summer the lemming nests underground.*

▶ *The European water vole spends less time in the water than muskrats and beavers, mainly burrowing in woods and meadows. It is almost less than half the size of voles living closer to the water.*

- **At the peak** of a lemming population explosion, lemmings devastate the local vegetation – and the next summer predators can find them more easily.

- **At 1 m below the snow's surface**, a lemming's winter nest can be 10°C, while outside it is below freezing.

- **Some species of voles and lemmings** have their first litters when they are only 5 weeks old themselves.

- **The collared lemming** is the only rodent to change the colour of its coat to white in winter.

- **Lemmings** will swim across any water in their path as they migrate in search of new food sources; if the water is too wide to cross, they drown – hence the myth of lemmings committing mass suicide.

- **A fox can hear** and smell voles moving under the snow.

Australian marsupials

- **The brush-tailed possum** is Australia's most common marsupial. It often moves into the lofts of houses.

- **Kangaroos** are not restricted to Australia – several tree-kangaroo species live in Papua New Guinea.

- **Australian marsupial moles** strongly resemble true moles, but have different ancestors.

- **Kangaroos are serious competitors** with sheep for grass, because with front teeth in both jaws, instead of just one, they crop it much closer.

▶ *The stocky wombat is related to the koala, but cannot climb trees and digs large burrows.*

- **Wombats** live in burrows and weigh up to 40 kg (but one fossil wombat weighed in at a hefty 100 kg).

- **The muscular tail** of the long-tailed dunnart is up to 210 mm long (twice its body length).

- **Unlike its cute appearance** the koala readily scratches and bites.

- **Australian marsupial moles** strongly resemble true moles, but have different ancestors.

- **The Australian pygmy possum** sleeps so soundly that you can pick it up without it waking.

- **The Tasmanian devil** is the largest surviving marsupial carnivore, eating mainly carrion.

▲ *The koala will spend almost all of its life in eucalyptus trees. Four hours a night will be spent on eating as much as 500g of leaves.*

Mole rats

- **Unlike most rodents**, mole rats live for several years.

- **Mole rats** have extremely loose skin, which enables them to turn round in the tightest of tunnels.

- **Naked mole rats** have no fur. They live in colonies, like some insects, with a queen that bears all the young, and workers that dig the tunnels.

▶ *Well equipped for subterranean life, mole rats will only surface to travel to another colony.*

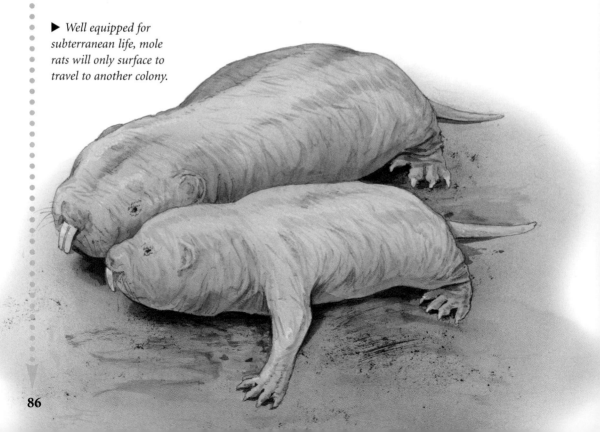

- **Mole rats**, unlike moles, dig with their protruding front teeth. Lip folds prevent them swallowing earth.

- **Mole rats' eyes** are probably blind, but they may use the eye surface to detect air currents in the burrow.

- **Mole rats** have been observed biting off the growing sprouts of roots and tubers before storing them, thus preventing them losing nutritive value before use.

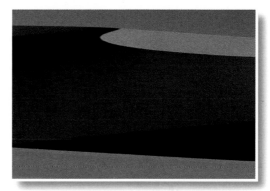

▲ *Naked mole rats enjoy stable temperatures of around 29°C in their humid burrows, when outside surface temperatures of the desert can be as high as 60°C.*

- **Blind mole rats** of the eastern Mediterranean have skin-covered eyes. They dig individual tunnel systems up to 350 m long.

- **Naked mole rats** cooperate to dig tunnels, several moving the soil to the surface and one kicking it out of the hole.

- **The Cape dune mole rat** moves up to half a tonne of soil in just 1 month.

> **. . .FASCINATING FACT. . .**
> The 'queen' of a naked mole rat colony
> suppresses the breeding ability of other
> females by means of chemical signals.

Gliders

- **Gliding mammals** include the flying squirrels of America and Asia, the scaly-tailed squirrels of Africa, and the marsupial gliding possums of Australia.

- **The Australian feather-tailed glider** is the smallest gliding mammal, weighing just 12 g.

- **Gliding mammals** achieve their glides by means of a hairy membrane called a patagium that joins the fore and hind limbs, and acts like a parachute.

- **The Southeast Asian colugo's** glide membrane stretches from the neck to fingers, toes and tail-tip.

- **When flying squirrels** come in to land on a tree trunk, they brake by turning their tail and body under, like the landing flaps on an aircraft's wing.

- **Africa's scaly-tailed flying squirrels** live in colonies of up to 100, and glide from tree to tree after dark.

▶ *The colugo (also known as a flying lemur) is about the size of a domestic cat. It has sharp claws for climbing and mottled fur for camouflage.*

- **Australia's gliders** feed on sap and gum, biting through tree bark and lapping up the sweet liquids.

- **Some flying squirrels**, when they land, quickly move to the opposite side of the tree trunk to avoid predators.

- **The colugo** is virtually helpless on the ground.

▶ *The southern flying squirrel fluffs out its tail and uses it as a rudder in mid-air.*

. . . **FASCINATING FACT** . . .
The longest glide by a gliding mammal ever recorded was 450 m by a giant flying squirrel.

Tenrecs and otter shrews

- **Tenrecs evolved** live on the island of Madagascar. Their physical appearance ranges from hedgehog look-alikes to shrews and web-footed otters.

- **Otter shrews**, close relatives to tenrecs, evolved separately on the African mainland. One species features in folklore as half mammal and half fish.

- **The body temperature** of tenrecs and otter shrews falls close to the surrounding air temperature while they are resting, enabling them to save energy.

- **The common tenrec** rears more young than any other mammal on the planet, with litters of up to 24.

- **The web-footed** tenrec was thought to be extinct, but is was recently re-discovered in the wild in Eastern Madagascar.

- **The insect-eating rice tenrec** resembles a mole, with its large front feet for digging and small eyes and ears.

- **The common tenrec**, weighing up to 1.5 kg, is the world's largest insectivore, and a ferocious fighter. It uses sharp neck spines to spike its attackers.

- **When alarmed**, baby common tenrecs rub together the quills on their backs to make a vibrating noise.

- **The aquatic otter shrews** of Africa use touch-sensitive whiskers to locate crabs and other prey.

... FASCINATING FACT ...
Some tenrecs find their way around at night by using a form of echolocation, based on a series of fast clicking noises made with the tongue.

◀ *Long-tailed tenrecs live in the forests of Madagascar.*

91

Mice

- **In the early 1940s**, a huge population of house mice in California had a density of about 200,000 per hectare.

- **The Andes fishing mouse** – only discovered in 1994 – fishes in streams at an altitude of at least 3,600 m.

- **The Australian pebble mound mouse** builds large piles of rounded stones, and then takes up residence in them.

- **The Oldfield mouse** has an escape tunnel leading from its nest near to the surface, so it can escape intruders by breaking through the apparent 'dead end'.

- **The water mice** of Central America have webbed, hairy feet that help them dive for water snails and fish.

- **American grasshopper mice** defend their territory by standing on their hind legs, shrieking at rival mice.

- **Grasshopper mice** are sometimes kept as pets to clear a house of insect pests such as cockroaches.

- **An ancient Greek legend** tells how a Cretan army owed its success to divine mice, which gnawed through the shield straps of the enemy.

- **The Old World harvest mouse** climbs through tall grasses using its grasping tail and flexible feet.

- **American kangaroo mice** have long, hairy hind feet and a long tail, and often travel in a series of leaps.

▶ *Though mice have small appetites they ruin vast amounts of food especially stores of grain.*

Burrowing house mouse

Yellow necked mouse

Climbing harvest mouse

Woodmouse

Striped field mouse

Spiny mouse

Wild pigs and peccaries

- **To obtain fruit** that is out of reach, African bush pigs will lean against fruit trees, making them topple over.

- **The warthog** uses its huge tusks for fighting and impressing other warthogs, not for digging for food – it feeds almost exclusively on grass.

- **The fleshy 'warts'** on a male warthog's face protect its eyes from tusk blows when it is fighting.

- **The largest wild pig**, at over 2 m long, is the African giant forest hog, which weighs in at 275 kg or more.

- **Pigs** were first domesticated at least 7000 years ago in southwest Asia.

▼ *Agile and powerful, the warthog forages across African woodlands and grasslands, often in family groups.*

◀ *The collared peccary also known as the javelina, has a fairly indistinct neck collar.*

- **The babirusa**, or pig-deer, of the Indonesian islands has four tusks, two of which pierce its flesh and grow through the top of its muzzle.

- **Peccaries**, the wild pigs of South America, have complex stomachs for digesting tough plant fibres.

- **Unlike other wild pigs**, peccaries live in herds which includes the adult males.

- **When a herd of peccaries** is attacked by a predator, a single peccary may confront the attacker, allowing the rest of the herd to escape.

> ...FASCINATING FACT...
> In 1975, the Chacoan peccary – known only from 10,000 year-old fossils – was found surviving in the forests of western Paraguay.

Bison

- **Hunters** on the Great Plains of North America reduced the number of bison from about 75 million to just a few hundred between about 1800 and 1900.

▲ *Bison compete mainly by threats, which may develop into full scale battles.*

- **Bison bulls compete** for herd leadership by charging at each other, and have developed enormously thick skulls to withstand the blows.

- **Bison** have such bad tempers that they cannot be trained in captivity.

- **The European bison**, or wisent, browses on forest leaves of oak, willow and elm, unlike its American relations, which graze on grass.

- **Standing up to 2 m high** at the shoulder, the European bison is the continent's largest wild animal.

- **The last truly wild** European bison was killed in 1919, but new herds – bred from zoo animals – have been established in reserves, in particular in the Bialowieza Forest in Poland.

- **In the 1800s**, the US Government approved the policy of killing bison in order to starve the Native Americans into submission.

- **The American plains bison** helped preserve the open prairies by eating the tree seedlings.

- **Saved by conservationists**, the American bison survives in small, managed herds in reservations and national parks.

- **Bison groom themselves** by rubbing their heads and bodies against tree trunks, and rolling in the dust.

▼ *Only a small percentage of the American bison population roam free in herds and most of these are within the boundaries of the national parks.*

97

Reindeer and caribou

▼ *Reindeer are the only deer in which both male and female have antlers.*

- **Reindeer** (Europe and Asia) and caribou (North America) are basically the same animal.

- **Reindeer** were probably first tamed in the 5th century AD by hunters, who used them as decoys when hunting wild reindeer.

- **The only females** in the deer family to have antlers are reindeer and caribou.

- **In 1984**, 10,000 migrating caribou drowned in Canada when dam sluices were opened.

- **Reindeer** have a well developed homing instinct, and can find their way even in blinding snowstorms.

- **Reindeer bulls fight with their feet** and rarely with their antlers, which could become locked together, leading to the starvation of both animals.

- **Reindeer are the best swimmers** of the deer family, due to the buoyancy of the hollow hairs of their coats.

- **Unlike other deer**, a reindeer's muzzle is covered in hair to help it forage in snow.

- **Reindeer dig** through the snow with their feet to find food.

◀ *European and Asian reindeer (shown here) have mainly grey top-coats, with fawn legs. American reindeer have brown coats with darker legs.*

⋯ **FASCINATING FACT** ⋯
The name 'caribou' means 'shoveller' in the language of one Canadian Indian people.

Sloth

- **The sloths of South America** have a variable body temperature, and each morning need to bask in the sun above the forest canopy.

- **The sloth** has the most neck vertebrae of any mammal, and can look forwards when it is upside down.

- **Sloths even mate** and give birth while hanging upside down by their powerful, curved claws.

- **Sloths' fur** grows in the opposite direction to that of most mammals, pointing towards the ground so the rain runs off the body.

- **A sloth's large stomach** is divided into many compartments; the food inside can account for up to a third of the animal's body weight.

- **A meal of leaves** may be retained in a sloth's digestive system for over a month.

▲ *The mother sloth carries her infant for up to 9 months on her belly, where it feeds on the leaves it can reach.*

▶ *This Lime's two toed sloth has two extremely long clawed toes on each of his front feet but three on each rear foot.*

- **The main predator** of the sloth is the harpy eagle.
- **Algae** grows in the grooves on a sloth's fur, helping to camouflage it in the forest greenery.
- **Sloths** have an amazing ability to heal themselves, and their wounds rarely become infected.
- **On land**, sloths can only move in an awkward, spread-eagled crawl, impeded by their claws.

Giraffes and okapis

- **The giraffe's black tongue** is almost 0.5 m long. It uses it to grip vegetation and pull it into its mouth.

- **The giraffe is the world's tallest animal** – some males reach up to 6 m in height.

- **Male giraffes stretch** up to reach leaves high in the trees, while females bend their necks to take lower leaves, thus reducing food competition.

- **Bony growths** on a male giraffe's skull continue to grow all its life, making its skull up to three times heavier than a female's.

- **The extraordinarily long necks** of giraffes have only 7 neck vertebrae, just like other mammals, but they are greatly elongated.

- **From a few weeks old**, young giraffes spend much of their time in a 'crèche', looked after by a pair of adults.

- **Female giraffes with calves** have been seen to beat severely and drive off attacking lions, using their hoofs, necks and heads as weapons.

▼ *Giraffes are swift runners and can reach speeds of over 50 km/h.*

- **To reach water**, giraffes have to spread their front legs wide apart. Special valves stop the blood rushing to and from their heads as they raise and lower them.

▲ *Giraffes spend much of the hot day feeding from acacia trees, shoots, fruits and vegetations. This is often referred to as 'browsing'.*

- **Okapis**, which are related to giraffes, closely resemble fossils of the giraffe's most recent ancestor, *Paleotragus*, from about 12 million years ago.

- **Okapis live so deep in the forests** of the Congo that they were not discovered by Europeans until the 1900s.

Sheep and goats

◀ *Domestic sheep have adapted to a life of migratory grazing, moving on as the grass is cropped.*

- **Despite their massive curled horns**, American bighorn rams fight predators with their feet.

- **The musk ox** of the Arctic tundra is more closely related to sheep and goats than to bison or oxen.

- **Sheep and goats** were domesticated as early as 7500 BC.

- **When young sheep and goats play**, they often leap onto their mothers' backs, practising for mountain life among the rocks.

- **Goats and sheep** have scent glands on their feet that mark mountain trails, helping herds stay together.

- **Bighorn rams** only fight with one another if their horns are of a similar size, ignoring larger or smaller rivals.

- **Avalanches** are the main threat to Rocky Mountain goats.

- **Of the two**, only sheep have scent glands on their faces, and only male goats have beards and a strong odour.

- **Central Asian argalis** are the largest Eurasian wild sheep, weighing up to 200 kg.

- **In a fight**, a European chamois may feign death to avoid being killed, lying flat with its neck outstretched.

▼ *Strong and healthy new born lambs are on their feet within minutes. Most lambs are born in early spring.*

Horses and asses

- **The earliest-known ancestor** of the horse, *Hyracotherium*, lived 50 million years ago, and was a forest dweller the size of a small dog.

- **Horses' earliest ancestors** evolved in America, and crossed land bridges to Asia and Europe, eventually becoming extinct in America.

- **A mule** is the offspring of a male ass and a female horse, while the rarer offspring of a male horse and female ass is called a hinny. Both mules and hinnies are unable to produce young.

- **Horses have very strong homing instincts**, and have been known to wander hundreds of kilometres to return to the place of their birth.

▼ *By nature horses are herd animals. In the wild a herd usually consists of one dominant stallion, accompanied by a number of mares and their young.*

- **The domestic horse** is the only member of the horse family in which the mane falls to the side – in all others, including asses and zebras, it stands erect.

- **Horses' eyes** are set high in the head and far apart, giving almost all round vision. They can focus on near and far objects at the same time.

- **The horse's large eyes** give it excellent night vision – almost as keen as that of owls.

- **Most horses sleep standing up** during the day, and at night sleep on the ground with their legs gathered under their bodies.

- **The earliest horses** had four toes per foot. These reduced as the horse moved from a forest to a plains life, and the modern horse has just a single toe.

▲ *The donkey evolved from African ass ancestors, and is capable of carrying heavy loads. All wild asses are desert dwellers, able to flourish on sparse vegetation.*

> **. . . . FASCINATING FACT. . . .**
> Horses were domesticated about 6000 years ago in Europe and Asia, mainly for their meat. They became transport animals from about 2000 BC.

107

Hippopotami

- **The lips of hippos** are up to 0.5 m wide, and contain strong muscles for grazing on short grasses.

- **Hippos** feed for 5 hours a night, and spend the next 19 hours resting in the water.

- **Hippos suckle their young** underwater and often sleep submerged, surfacing regularly to breath whilst still unconscious.

▼ *The Hippopotamus has a huge head with a large mouth well equipped with strong teeth, of which the canine set form the massive tusks.*

- **A pygmy hippo** is born on land in just 2 minutes, and has to be taught how to swim.

- **In dry air** the pygmy hippo loses water by evaporation at about five times the rate of human water loss.

- **Hippos travel** up to 30 km at night in search of food, but if frightened will run back to water to hide.

- **Hippos** are probably Africa's most dangerous animal. They kill a large number of humans each year.

- **Bull hippos** mark their territory by scattering dung with their whirling tails.

- **Aggressive hippos** warn off other hippos by opening their jaws to display their formidable tusks. They regularly fight to the death.

- **Male hippos** can weigh as much as 3200 kg.

▲ *Calves stay with their mothers well after weaning, until about 4-5 years. The family group form a very close bonding.*

Rabbits and hares

- **Hares** are born with fur, with their eyes open; rabbits are born naked, with eyes shut.

- **Mother hares** visit their young for just five minutes a day to feed them on their rich milk.

▼ *The snowshoe hare's large eyes help it see during dusk and after dark, when it is most active.*

- **Snowshoe hares** have broad, hairy hind feet for moving over snow.

- **If a hare sees it is being stalked** by a fox, it stands up to put the fox off a chase (which the hare would win).

- **The pikas** of Asia and western America 'sing' loudly.

- **Rabbits' incisors** grow constantly.

- **Both sexes** of hares 'box' as part of the mating ritual.

- **Hares** can reach speeds of up to 60 km/h when running flat out.

- **Large-eared pika** is one of the highest-living mammal in the world, inhabiting mountain ranges in Asia at altitudes up to 6130 m.

▲ *Rabbits, like hares, can close and open their slitlike nostrils at will.*

... FASCINATING FACT ...
Numbers of American snowshoe hares rise and fall in an 8-11 year cycle, affecting the numbers of lynxes, which depend on them as food.

Elephants

- **The name 'elephant'** means 'visible from afar'.

- **Elephants communicate** over great distances by making low frequency sounds (too low for humans to hear).

- **War elephants** were used by the Carthaginian general Hannibal against the Romans in the 3rd century BC, and by the Romans invading Britain in the 1st century AD.

- **Elephants sometimes enter caves** to excavate minerals such as sodium, needed as a supplement to their diet.

- **Elephants** spend up to 18 hours a day feeding.

▼ *An elephant's trunk is a combination of upper lip and nose, and is used to place food into its mouth. It also doubles as a hose, squirting water down its throat and acting as a shower spray.*

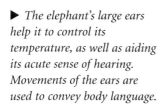

▶ *The elephant's large ears help it to control its temperature, as well as aiding its acute sense of hearing. Movements of the ears are used to convey body language.*

- **Elephants are good swimmers** – some Asian elephants have been seen to swim non-stop for as much as 10 km.

- **Asian elephants** are the world's longest-lived mammals after humans, and can live to be over 70 years.

- **An African elephant** needs to eat up to 6% of its bodyweight each day – 300 kg for a 5000 kg bull!

- **An elephant uses eight grinding teeth** at any one time. The teeth are replaced as they wear out – it gets through up to 48 during its lifetime.

... **FASCINATING FACT** ...
Stone Age rock paintings in North Africa show that elephants once lived in the Sahara region, before it became desert.

113

Rhinoceros

- **The Sumatran rhino** is a relative of the woolly rhinoceros of the last Ice Age, and has reddish fur.

- **When black rhinos** are fleeing, the calf follows the mother, but when white rhinos are in flight, the mother runs behind the calf.

▲ *The rhino has one or two horns, depending on species, perched on a tough area of the skull. They are made of solid keratin and are extremely heavy.*

- **African ox-birds** ride aboard rhinos, cleaning out ticks from the folds in their hides.

- **Despite weighing 2 tonnes** or more, the rhino can run at 50 km/h, and make a 180° turn within its own body length.

- **If two rhinos feel threatened**, they stand back to back, confronting their enemies from different directions.

- **Rhinos can be heard** munching on plants from a distance of 400 m.

- **The upper lips** of the African white rhino are square, for grazing on grass; those of the African black rhino are pointed, for plucking leaves.

- **Rhinos have poor eyesight**, and cannot locate a motionless object further than 30 m away.

- **A prehistoric relative** of the rhinoceros, *Indricotherium*, stood 5.4 m tall and weighed 20 tonnes.

- **Thicker skin** on a rhino's flanks protect it from horn wounds from rivals.

▶ *The rhino has excellent hearing through his tubular ears.*

Old World camels

- **Single-humped dromedaries** and twin-humped Bactrian camels can go for months without food and water, living on the fat in their humps.

- **A female dromedary** can produce 6 litres of milk a day for 9 to 18 months – the staple food for some camel-herding peoples.

- **After not drinking for many months**, a camel can drink up to 130 litres in just a few minutes.

- **Unlike other mammals**, camels have oval instead of round blood-cells. These prevent their blood thickening as their body temperature rises.

- **Evolving originally in North America**, some camel ancestors crossed land bridges to Asia to become today's Bactrian camels and dromedaries.

- **Introduced to Australia** as desert transport animals, dromedaries reverted to the wild there.

- **Domesticated in Arabia** some 6000 years ago, the dromedary, or Arabian camel, ceased to exist in the wild about 2000 years ago.

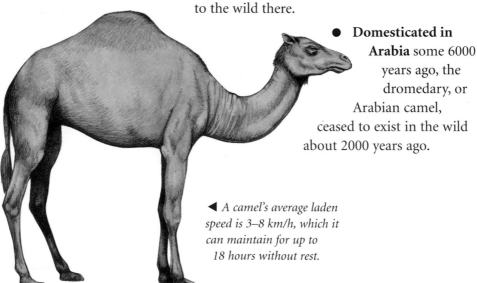

◀ *A camel's average laden speed is 3–8 km/h, which it can maintain for up to 18 hours without rest.*

- **Camels do sweat**, but not until their body temperature has reached 40.5°C.

- **In the annual King's Camel Race** in Saudi Arabia, some 3000 camels are raced over a 23 km course.

- **Only about 1000** wild Bactrian camels survive, in Mongolia's Gobi Desert.

▼ *These dromedary camels are well suited to life in hot climates. They have broad feet to keep them steady on desert sand along with slitlike nostrils and long eylashes to protect them during sand storms.*

Monotremes

- **Monotremes** are egg-laying mammals. There are only two groups: the duckbilled platypus of Australia and the echidna, or spiny anteater, of Australia and New Guinea.

- **If harassed** on soft ground by a predator, the echidna digs down until only an area of spines is showing.

- **The platypus** is the only known mammal to detect the electric fields of its prey by means of electro-receptors in its muzzle.

- **Hunting underwater** with eyes and ears closed, the platypus eats up to 30% of its own weight each day.

- **The female echidna** has a pouch in which the young develop after hatching from their egg.

- **Poison** from the spurs on the male platypus's hind ankles can kill a dog within minutes.

▶ *In the breeding season the female echidna develops a temporary pouch on her stomach. After she lays her egg she transfers it into the pouch for incubation, which lasts about 8–9 days.*

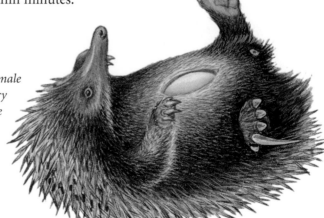

- **Before the discovery** of fossil platypus teeth in Argentina, the animal was believed only to have existed in Australia and New Guinea.

- **The platypus loses its teeth** a few weeks after birth, and thereafter grinds its food with special mouth pads.

- **The platypus's burrow** can extend 30 m from the water's edge to the nest. It blocks the entrance to deter snakes.

◄ *The duckbilled platypus swims mainly with its front legs, trailing its rear legs as a rudder.*

...**FASCINATING FACT**...
The duckbilled platypus lives almost all its life either underwater or underground.

119

Tapirs

- **The forest-dwelling tapirs** of Asia and America are related to horses and rhinos, and probably resemble early horses.

- **Tapirs** moved across land bridges from North America to South America and Asia over 5 million years ago.

- **The Malayan tapir** has stark black and white colouring that breaks up its body outline in moonlit forests.

- **Tapirs use their long snouts as snorkels**, staying underwater for several minutes to elude predators.

- **All newly born tapirs** have the same stripes and spots, which fade away within six months.

- **The South American mountain tapir** grazes at altitudes of over 5000 m.

- **The earliest-known tapir** lived some 55 million years ago.

▼ *This Brazilian tapir spends most of its time in water with just its trunk sticking out rather like a snorkel.*

- **Tapirs, horses and rhinos** are the only living members of the Perissodactyla order of mammals, with an uneven number of toes per foot.

- **In South America**, engineers have built roads along ancient tapir trails, which accurately follow land contours.

▼ *The Malayan tapir eats the young shoots of rubber trees.*

> **... FASCINATING FACT ...**
> The Malayan tapir walks along the bottom
> of rivers and lakes like a hippopotamus.

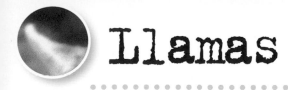

Llamas

- **The Inca people** of Peru (whose empire lasted from 1400 to 1533) domesticated llamas and alpacas, but were unable to tame the vicuña.

- **Vicuña herds** defend two permanent territories, one where they feed, and a smaller one at a higher altitude where they sleep at night.

- **The Incas** used llamas to carry secret messages tied into their fur.

- **Vicuñas** can live at altitudes of 5486 m, where the air is too thin for most mammals.

- **Unlike** in other hoofed mammals, vicuñas' incisor teeth never stop growing.

▼ *These llamas have been raised by Andean people mainly for their fine wool.*

- **Fine vicuña wool** was reserved for the robes of the Inca royal family and their nobles.

- **When annoyed**, llamas spit at their opponents, sometimes including a pebble as a missile in with their saliva.

- **Llama herders** use the animals' fur for rugs and ropes, their hides for shoe leather, their fat for candles, their dung for fuel, and their milk and flesh for food.

- **Baby llamas** can get up and follow their mothers just 15–30 minutes after being born.

▲ *Domestic llamas are usually mild-tempered, but still spit to show their anger.*

> **...FASCINATING FACT...**
> A llama can carry a 60-kg load up to 30 km
> a day across high mountainous terrain.

Pandas

- **In the late 1900s**, many pandas starved to death because the fountain bamboo they ate came to the end of its 100-year growth cycle and died back.

- **Giant pandas** often give birth to twins, but in the wild one cub is always left to die.

- **Pandas** have an inefficient digestive system – up to 50% of the plant material they eat passes out of the body intact within 10 hours.

- **Although bamboo** forms the bulk of its diet, the giant panda also eats fish, small birds and rodents.

◀ *The giant panda eats sitting up, pushing bamboo canes into its mouth for 16 hours a day.*

- **In ancient China**, pandas were believed to have magical powers, and people wore panda masks to ward off evil spirits.

- **Reduced in number** by hunting and deforestation, there are probably fewer than 1000 giant pandas left in the wild, in forest reserves in southeast China.

- **The giant panda** has an unsuccessful zoo breeding record, with about 20 successes in the last 50 years.

- **Much livelier** than the giant panda, the red panda is a nimble climber. It uses its long tail for balance, and when threatened rears up and hisses.

- **Giant pandas** reach up to 150 kg in weight, but when new-born weigh only 100–150 g.

> ...**FASCINATING FACT**...
> Giant and red pandas have an extra 'thumb'
> that enables them to grasp their food.

◀ *The panda's diet is almost 99% bamboo. Eating fresh shoots in spring, mature leaves in summer and stems in winter. Bamboo thickets also provide shelter for sleeping.*

125

Domestic cattle

- **European domestic cattle** are descended from the aurochs, a large wild ox seen in ancient cave drawings.

- **The wild auroch** was domesticated about 6500 BC.

- **Humped zebu** are the main domestic cattle of Asia.

- **In India**, zebu are considered holy by Hindus, and are allowed to roam free, eat fruit off market stalls, and sleep in the roads.

▼ *Wild ancestors of modern European cattle were domesticated, mainly for milk, some 8500 years ago by nomadic tribes-people.*

▶ *Dairy cows give birth to one calf a year and if milked regularly can go on to produce 9–15 litres of milk a day for the following ten months.*

- **Domesticated water buffalo** in Egypt, India and Southeast Asia are powerful draught animals, and are also regularly milked.

- **India** is the country with the most domestic cattle: more than 270 million.

- **A large feral population** of domesticated water buffalo lives in northern Australia.

- **Masai cattle herders** in Kenya regularly take blood from the throats of their cattle and drink it.

- **In Tibet,** domesticated yaks thrive at altitudes well over 6000 m, providing meat, milk and transport.

- **Domestic cattle** sleep for up to 8 minutes at a time, for a maximum total of 60 minutes in 24 hours.

127

Kangaroos

- **Female kangaroos** suckling young of different ages at the same time are able to produce milk of different concentrations for the individual youngsters.

- **Hopping** is a good way to travel fast, but to go slowly a kangaroo has to use its tail as a fifth supporting leg.

- **Some tree kangaroos** can leap to the ground from as high as 30 m without coming to harm.

- **New-born kangaroos** are deaf as well as naked and blind.

- **Flat out**, some kangaroos can reach a speed of almost 65 km/h, making huge hops of over 8 m in length.

- **When bounding**, most kangaroos can only move their hind legs both at the same time, but when swimming can move them alternately.

- **Hare wallabies** are small members of the kangaroo family weighing only 1–4.5 kg.

◀ *The baby kangaroo becomes independent after spending almost 190 days in its mother's pouch.*

- **Rock wallabies** live on rocky outcrops. Their rough-soled feet are fringed with stiff hairs, enabling them to climb steep rock faces.

- **When male kangaroos fight**, they support themselves on their tails and deliver slashing kicks with their hind legs.

▲ *A moving kangaroo uses its large, muscular tail as a counter-balance.*

....FASCINATING FACT...
Prehistoric kangaroos in Australia included a giant that stood 2.4 m tall and weighed 270 kg, and at least one meat-eating species.

Moose and elk

● **The world's largest deer** (called moose in North America and elk in Europe) stand up to 2 m tall at the shoulder.

▲ *Two male elk spar with their antlers, which they lose and regain every year.*

● **Moose escape wolves** by retreating to marshes and lakes, but in winter the wolves can follow them across the ice.

● **The prehistoric Irish elk**, which became extinct 10,000 years ago, had massive antlers up to 4.3 m across.

● **Moose** have reached Isle Royale in Lake Superior, USA, by swimming across 32 km of water.

● **To protect her calf** from wolves, the mother moose shepherds it into shallow water and stands between it and the wolves, which usually give up.

- **A moose will use its great weight** to push over young trees to get at twigs and shoots.

- **A moose eats** the equivalent of 20,000 leaves a day.

- **The antlers** of a moose are 'palmate', with broad areas like hands.

- **A young moose** stays with its mother for almost a year, but she chases it away just before she is about to give birth to a new calf.

▼ *Following a gestation period of nine months this female moose will normally give birth to a single calf, but occasionally twins.*

> ...**FASCINATING FACT**...
> The moose has been known to dive to 5.5 m, staying under water for 30 seconds, to reach water plants and roots.

Prehistoric elephants

- *Platybelodon*, which lived up to 14 million years ago, had huge, shovel-like lower teeth for scooping up and cutting water plants, and a short, broad trunk.

- **Remains of 91-cm tall elephants** were found on Malta.

- **The last woolly mammoths** were a dwarf species that died out less than 7000 years ago.

- **Two million years ago**, *Deinotherium* may have used its curled tusks for scraping bark from trees.

- **The elephant *Gomphotheres*** had four straight tusks, and lived in Europe, Africa and Pakistan.

- **Forest-dwelling *Anancus*** had straight tusks up to 4 m long, which it used for digging up roots.

- **At one time**, more commercial ivory came from frozen mammoths in Siberia than from modern elephants.

- **Some Stone Age Siberian people** built huts from the tusks and long bones of the mammoths they hunted.

- **Mastodons** had smaller bodies and tusks than mammoths, and had a different diet.

◀ The *Anancas was well equipped with long tusks for digging up roots.*

▶ Platybelodon *was a swamp elephant that devoured huge amounts of water plants, scooping them up with its lower jaw.*

... FASCINATING FACT ...
One of the earliest-known elephant ancestors, *Moeritherium*, lived about 38 million years ago.

133

Buffaloes

- **The African buffalo** will stalk and attack a human even if unprovoked, and will mob lions and kill their cubs if it gets the chance.

- **The wild Asiatic buffalo** can weigh up to 1200 kg, and has the longest horns of any living animal, sometimes exceeding a 4-m spread.

- **African buffaloes** have a wide range of vocal communications, including signals for moving off, direction-changing, danger and aggressive intent.

- **In Australia in the dry season**, female feral water buffaloes leave their calves with a 'nursemaid' on the edge of the plains where they graze.

- **The African savannah buffalo** can weigh up to 875 kg, and herds can number several thousand.

- **A wounded African buffalo** will ambush its hunter, exploding out of cover in an unstoppable charge.

▼ *African buffaloes gather together in herds of over 2000. The largest male will dominate the smaller and female buffaloes.*

- **Needing to drink every day**, African buffaloes never stray more than 15 km from water.

▲ Swamp mud helps protect a water buffalo's skin from heat and insects.

- **Buffaloes rarely fight**. Contests consist of tossing the head, pawing the ground and circling, before one bull walks away.

- **Blind or crippled buffaloes** are sometimes observed living healthily in the herd, whereas loners would soon die.

- **In the rinderpest cattle epidemic** of the 1890s, up to 10,000 African buffaloes died for every one animal that survived.

Koalas

- **Koala numbers** started to rise after European settlers reduced the numbers of dingoes.

- **Male koalas mark their territories** by rubbing their large chest gland, which females lack, onto tree trunks.

- **The koala feeds** mainly on eucalyptus leaves.

- **Koalas** are the sole living representatives of their family, but are distantly related to wombats.

- **The koala grips branches** with its sharp-clawed hands by opposing the first two fingers to the other three.

- **Koalas spend 80% of their day** asleep in the trees.

- **When its body temperature** nears 37°C, the koala licks its paws and rubs cooling saliva onto its face.

- **The name 'koala'** comes from an Aboriginal word meaning 'no drink' – it gets most of the moisture it needs from the leaves it eats.

- **A giant koala**, twice the size of today's animals, existed over 40,000 years ago.

> ...**FASCINATING FACT**...
> A koala weighs less than 0.5 g at birth, and remains in its mother's pouch for 7 months.

▶ *Although resembling a bear, koalas are not related to the bear family.*

Fruit bats

▶ *Unlike echolocating bats, fruit bats, navigate visually, and live on a plant diet.*

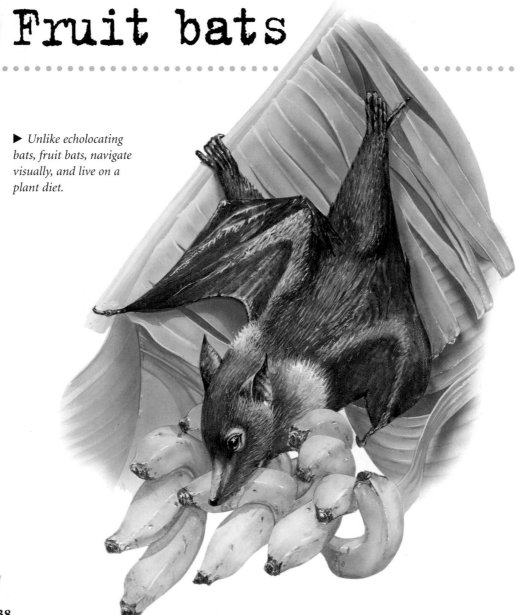

- **In Southwest Asia,** some date farmers protect their fruit from fruit bat raiders by covering the dates with bags of woven palm leaves.

- **Island fruit bats** are vulnerable to tropical storms that can blow them far out to sea. This is how some species reached islands in the first place.

- **Fruit bats** enjoy eating fruit in mangrove forests, where sea-water minerals supplement their diet.

- **Large fruit bats** strip the leaves from the trees in which they roost to give them a clearer view.

- **Male hammer-headed bats** gather together in riverside trees called leks, so that the females can choose a mate from among them. As they hang, the males flap their wings and call out.

- **The Queensland tube-nosed bat** has tube-like nostrils projecting 5–6 mm from its face. These may act as snorkels as it feeds on pulpy fruit.

- **Fruit bats eat their own weight** in fruit each day, and are important seed-dispersers, spitting out seeds as they eat.

- **Australian black fruit bats** chew leaves to get protein, but spit them out after swallowing the juice to make flying easier.

- **Spectacled flying foxes** sometimes drink sea-water as they skim by, and have been snapped up by saltwater crocodiles.

...FASCINATING FACT...
The largest fruit bat is the Indian flying fox,
which has a wingspan of up to 150 cm.

Gazelles and antelopes

- **The smallest antelope**, the West African royal antelope, is only the size of a brown hare, and weighs between 1.5 and 3 kg.

- **When the Indian blackbuck antelope** runs flat out, it reaches 80 km/h, making 8-m long strides. The Indian aristocracy once used trained cheetahs to hunt them.

▼ *The Indian blackbuck is one of the world's fastest animals, with entire herds travelling at up to 80 km/h.*

- **When a dominant greater kudu bull lies down**, he suddenly loses all authority, and female and young bull kudus often harass and annoy him with impunity.

- **The giant eland** of West and Central Africa is the largest of all antelopes, reaching 3.5 m in length, 1.85 m at the shoulder, and weighing up to 940 kg.

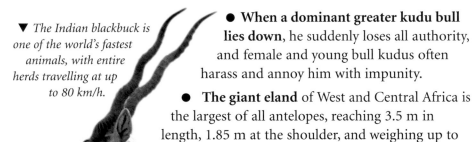

▲ *A fleeing springbok may leap vertically in an activity known as 'pronking', confusing predators and giving the springbok a better view.*

- **The American pronghorn antelope** has been timed running at 56 km/h for 6 km, and up to 88.5 km/h over short distances less than 1 km.

- **When migrating** to new grazing grounds, herds of wildebeest sometimes number up to 1.3 million individuals, and the herd may measure as much as 40 km in length.

- **The Arabian oryx** is a desert specialist, with a pale, heat-reflecting coat and splayed hoofs for walking in soft sand. Its small size enables it to shelter in the shade of shrubby trees.

- **The spiral-horned antelopes**, which include elands, kudus and bongos, are found only in Africa, and are an offshoot of the ancestors of domestic cattle.

- **The springbok** is famous for its spectacular, stiff-legged leaps while running.

......FASCINATING FACT......
Impalas can make leaps 3 m high and 11 m long when startled by a predator.

141

Deer and chevrotains

- **The tiny Chinese water deer** is unique in the deer family in that it gives birth to as many as seven fawns at a time.

- **Chevrotains**, or mouse-deer, are in a separate family from true deer. They eat fish and meat as well as plants.

- **Reindeer** are the only deer species in which the females have antlers, using them to find moss under the snow.

▼ *Deer have large, mobile ears that are constantly alert.*

- **Male musk deer** use their long, down-curved canine teeth when fighting rival males in the mating season.

- **The antlers** that male deer use for fighting are shed each year, regrowing the following spring.

- **Indian chital deer** seek out langur monkeys, feeding on the leafy stems thrown down by the monkeys above.

- **When competing for females**, red deer stags prefer to roar at each other rather than fight and risk an injury.

- **Newly grown antlers** are covered with a protective skin known as 'velvet', which stags rub off against trees.

- **On the Scottish island of Rhum**, red deer supplement their plant diet by snacking on Manx shearwater chicks.

▲ *The chevrotain, sometimes known as the mouse deer, is probably related to pigs and camels.*

> ...FASCINATING FACT...
> In the Middle Ages, the kings of Europe planted royal forests specially for deer-hunting.

143

Zebras

◀ *The zebra has a small bristly mane which stands erect, running down the back of its neck. The female gives birth to a single foal, occasionally twins, after a gestation period of up to a year.*

- **A zebra's stripes** are as individual as human fingerprints – no two zebras are exactly the same.

- **The quagga** was a South African zebra that only had stripes on the front part of its body.

- **The home range** of Grevy's zebra, which roams desert and savannah terrains in northeastern Kenya, sometimes exceeds 10,000 sq km.

- **The zebra** can be a formidable foe, driving off lions, and even killing humans to defend its foals.

- **The plains zebra** lived north of the Sahara, in Algeria and Tunisia, up until 10,000 years ago, when it was replaced by the African wild ass.

- **Grevy's zebra** is a large species with narrowly spaced stripes and very large, mule-like ears.

- **A plains zebra herd's stallion** will challenge any potential rival coming within 50–100 m of his herd.

- **The quagga** once existed in very large herds, but became extinct through over-hunting in the 1870s.

- **Mountain zebras** follow ancient trails to mountain springs and pools in the dry season, and dig for subsurface water in stream beds.

- **Chapman's zebra** has shadow stripes – light, greyish stripes that alternate with the dark main stripes.

▼ *Zebras are sociable and like physical contact and mutual grooming*

Sea otters

- **Sea otters** live in the northeastern Pacific. They rarely come ashore, and sleep floating on their backs, wrapped in kelp seaweed to stop them drifting away.

- **The sea otter's thick fur** – the densest of any mammal in the world – keeps it warm in cold waters.

- **The heaviest** of all otters, the sea otter weighs up to 45 kg and reaches up to 1.4 m from nose to tail.

- **To maintain warmth and energy**, the sea otter eats up to 30% of its total weight each day, diving repeatedly for shellfish, sea urchins and octopi.

▼ *Sea otters are sociable creatures, living
in groups and coming ashore only rarely.*

▶ *The sea otter uses both its front paws to hold food while floating on its back.*

- **The sea otter** was the most recent mammal to evolve from a life on land to one in the sea.

- **In the 1700s and 1800s**, sea otters were hunted almost to extinction for their valuable fur, which was known as 'soft gold'.

- **To crack open shells**, the sea otter lies on its back and balances a rock on its stomach, using it like an anvil.

- **Sea otters** sleep, socialize and give birth on kelp beds.

- **Unique among otters**, sea otters can extend and contract the claws of their front feet, like a cat.

- **People have seen** sea otters bite open old drinks cans from the seabed to get at octopi hiding inside.

147

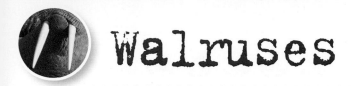

Walruses

- **A single walrus tusk** can measure up to 1 m long and weigh 5.4 kg.

- **Walruses swim** by sweeping their huge rear flippers from side to side, each one opening in turn like a 1-m wide fan.

- **The walrus is protected from the cold** by a thick layer of blubber – a third of its total weight.

- **In the summer**, basking walruses turn a deep pink as their blood vessels dilate to radiate heat away from the body.

- **Walruses** excavate shellfish from seabed mud by squirting a high-pressure blast of water from their mouths.

- **The walrus has 300 whiskers** on each side of its moustache, which it uses to help it find food in murky waters.

- **A walrus uses its long tusks** to help it clamber onto ice floes – its scientific name, *Odobenus*, means 'tooth walker'.

- **In water**, a walrus turns a pale grey colour as blood leaves its skin to maintain the temperature of its body core.

- **A walrus can eat** 3000 clams in one day.

◄ *Walruses are very sociable, and like to gather in huge groups on coastal ice or rocks.*

▶ *A walrus's tusks are actually extra-long upper canine teeth. The tusks of the male are longer, and used both for display and for competing with rivals during the breeding season.*

. . . **FASCINATING FACT** . . .
Walrus pups are born 15 months after the parents have mated – 4 to 5 months pass before the egg starts to grow in the mother's womb.

Seals

▲ *The elephant seal frequents the icy waters of the Antarctic,*
living in social groups and feeding on fish and squid.

- **When chasing penguins,** the leopard seal can leap 2 m from the sea onto an ice floe.

- **Male southern elephant seals,** which weigh up to 3500 kg, have inflatable snouts used to impress females during mating displays.

- **In the 4 days after being born,** hooded seal pups double their weight from 25 kg to 50 kg.

- **The elephant seal** can dive as deep as 1500 m, and can stay under water for 1–2 hours.

- **Leopard seals** are the only seals known to make unprovoked attacks on humans, lunging through ice to get at their feet.

- **Seals can sleep** floating vertically in the water just beneath the surface, rising occasionally to breathe through their nostrils.

- **When a seal dives deep**, its heartbeat slows from 55–120 beats per minute to 4–15 beats per min.

- **Crab-eater seals** have special teeth that they use like strainers to catch the shrimp-like krill on which they feed.

- **The fur seals** of the North Pacific spend up to 8 months of the year continuously at sea, feeding.

▼ *Leopard seals are solitary and aggressive. They have clawed front flippers and prey on penguins, birds and even smaller seals.*

...**FASCINATING FACT**...
The world's largest mammal herd consists of up to 1.5 million northern fur seals, which breed on two islands in the Pacific sub-Arctic region.

151

Manatees and dugongs

- **Manatees and dugongs**, known as sirenians, are the only vegetarian sea mammals in the world.

- **In the days of sail**, sailors sometimes mistook manatees, which can float upright in the water, for mermaids.

- **About 90% of Florida's manatees** carry scars on their bodies caused by power-boat propellers.

- **Manatees** are very slow breeders, and currently more die each year than are born, threatening their extinction.

- **Manatees** have been used successfully to clear waterways of the fast-growing water hyacinth.

- **Stella's seacow** was a massive North Pacific sirenian, up to 9 m long and weighing 6400 kg. It was hunted to extinction in the 18th century.

- **Fossil evidence** shows that manatees and dugongs have existed for about 50 million years (much longer than seals). They are probably related to elephants.

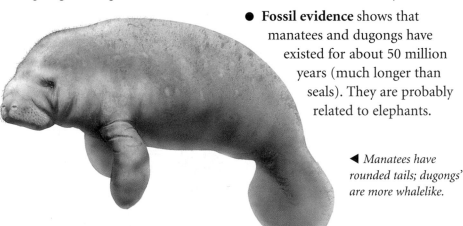

◄ *Manatees have rounded tails; dugongs' are more whalelike.*

152

- **The teeth of manatees** are regularly replaced, being shed at the front as they wear out, and replaced by new ones moving forward.

- **Amazonian manatees**, found only in the Amazon River and its tributaries, fast during the 6-month dry season.

- **The dugong** of the Indian Ocean and South Pacific feeds entirely on eel grass, which is the only flowering marine plant.

▶ *Manatee numbers are around 130,000 – their only enemies are humans.*

153

Toothed whales

- **Beluga whales** are the only white whales. They were once called 'sea canaries' by seamen, because their bird-like calls can be heard above the water's surface.

- **Sperm whales** will form a defensive circle, heads to the centre, around young or wounded group members, and beat off predators with their tails.

- **Beaked whales** feed mainly on cuttlefish and squid – one bottle-nosed whale was found to have the remains of 10,000 cuttlefish in its stomach.

- **All dolphins are toothed whales.** The orca – the largest member of the dolphin family – half-beaches itself to catch seals at the water's edge.

- **Beaked whales will dive to 500 m** or more to escape orcas, staying in the depths for an hour or more until the danger has passed.

- **Spending 85% of the day** under the sea's surface, bottle-nosed whales have been recorded diving to well over 1500 m in their search for their squid prey.

▼ *Killer whales are highly sociable creatures, living in family groups known as pods.*

Extremely tall dorsal fin (straight and vertical in males, curved in females)

Pale markings help break up the body's outline

▲ *As the sperm whale surfaces, it pushes out stale air through its blowhole.*

- **Beluga whales** are frequently stranded in coastal shallows as the tide retreats, and wait patiently for the next tide to refloat them.

- **The massive sperm whale**, which weighs up to 70 tonnes, has the largest brain of any mammal on Earth. Fat deposits in its brain case help to focus the sounds the whale produces by echolocation.

- **Toothed whales** cooperate with one another far more than baleen whales do, often working together to herd prey into a tight mass for easy feeding.

...**FASCINATING FACT**...
The male strap-toothed whale has two teeth in its lower jaw that grow to wrap around its upper jaw, severely restricting its ability to open its beak-like mouth.

Dolphins

◀ *The Atlantic humpback dolphin inhabits mainly shallower waters, but is also known to swim close to fishing boats where it can feed on the rich shoals.*

- **Groups of common dolphins**, travelling and feeding together, may number up to 2000 individuals.

- **Orcas,** or killer whales, are actually the largest species of dolphin, though they feed on other dolphin species.

- **There are five species** of freshwater dolphin living in Asian and South American rivers. Most catch fish by sound rather than sight.

- **Dolphins** have been known to aid humans by keeping them afloat and driving off attacking sharks.

- **Spinner dolphins** are named for the acrobatic leaps they perform, spinning up to seven times in mid air.

- **The Atlantic hump-backed dolphin** helps fishermen in West Africa by driving shoals of mullet into their nets.

- **In Mexico's Baja California**, bottle-nosed dolphins chase fish up onto the shore, then roll up onto the beach, completely out of the water, to grab them.

- **Military observers** once recorded a group of dolphins swimming at 64 km/h in the bow wave of a warship.

- **The striped dolphin**, seen in ancient Greek paintings, leaps up to 7 m to perform somersaults and spins.

- **The Yangtse dolphin**, or baiji, is one of the world's rarest mammals – probably less than 300 survive.

▼ *Many dolphin species 'spy-hop'. holding their heads out of the water as they check on their surroundings for predators and potential food.*

Baleen whales

- **Baleen whales** include blue whales, the planet's largest mammals – the heaviest known weighed over 190 tonnes.

- **Blue whale calves** grow about 1000 times faster in the womb than human babies.

- **Humpback whales** have been seen to leap out of the water as many as 100 times in quick succession.

- **Right whales** were so-named because they were the 'right' ones to hunt – heavy with oil, meat and baleen.

▶ *The plated lower jaws of baleen whales take in masses of water per gulp.*

◄ *Humpback whales may weigh up to 30 tonnes, yet they are able to 'breach' out of the water using their powerful tail.*

- **Despite being protected** since the 1940s, there are less than 320 northern right whales surviving.

- **The baleen plates** of modern baleen whales evolved about 30 million years ago.

- **Right whales** force a constant current of water through their baleen plates to trap their food – krill organisms.

- **Bowhead whales** are estimated to eat up to 1500 kg of filtered-out food organisms daily for 130 days at a time.

- **Women's corsets** were once made out of baleen plates.

> ...**FASCINATING FACT**...
> Humpback whales produce columns of air bubbles that force their prey into clusters.

Orang-utans

▲ *Orang-utans are slow breeders, and may only give birth to three or four babies in a lifetime.*

- **Orang-utans** spend much more time in trees than the other great apes, and are the largest tree-dwelling mammals in the world.

- **Insatiable eaters**, orang-utans can spend an entire day feasting in one heavily laden fruit tree.

- **The name 'orang-utan'** means 'man of the forest' in the language of the local tribespeople of Southeast Asia.

- **A mature male orang-utan** makes his presence known to other orang-utans by breaking branches, bellowing and groaning. Local legends explain this as a sign of the ape's grief over losing a human bride.

- **In Sumatra,** the major predators of orang-utans are tigers at ground level, and clouded leopards in trees.

- **Once found all over Southeast Asia,** orang-utans now live only in tropical Borneo and Sumatra.

- **Like chimpanzees,** orang-utans use sticks as tools to retrieve food from crevices and to scratch themselves.

▲ *Young orang-utans stay with their mothers until they are about eight years old.*

- **Male orang-utans** have large air sacs that extend from their throats, under their arms and over their shoulders, and increase the loudness and range of their calls.

- **To help her young** move from tree to tree, a mother orang-utan pulls the branches of two trees closer together and makes a bridge with her body.

- **Orang-utans make a nest** at night, building a roof to keep off the rain.

161

Gorillas

- **Male gorillas walk on four limbs** most of the time, but will run on two legs for short distances, beating their chests, when showing off.

- **Adult gorillas** sleep in a new nest every night.

- **The mature male leader** of a gorilla group is called a 'silverback', after the saddle of white hair on its back.

- **Young male gorillas** form their own groups by kidnapping females from other groups.

- **Mountain gorillas** spend almost all their lives at 2800 to 3400 m above sea level, in damp, cloudy conditions.

▼ *The male gorilla is far larger than the female, and is the largest of all the primates – big silverbacks can weigh as much as 200 kg.*

◀ *The bond between a mother gorilla and her young is very strong. Babies are not properly weaned until they are three years old, but may stay with the mother for another year, or until another baby has been born.*

- **Some gorillas supplement their plant diet** by eating handfuls of potassium- and calcium-rich soil.

- **If a gorilla cannot keep up** with the group because of a wound, the silverback slows down so it is not left behind.

- **When aggressive male gorillas** beat their chests and mock-charge one another, they give off an armpit odour powerful enough to be detected 25 m away by humans.

- **Despite their huge strength**, silverbacks are gentle with their offspring, allowing them to play on their backs.

> ...**FASCINATING FACT**...
> The 'nose-prints' of gorillas are as distinctive as human fingerprints – no two are identical.

163

Old World monkeys

- **Japanese macaques** sit in hot springs in winter to keep warm.
- **Some female red colobus monkeys** in Gambia gang up to attack, and even kill, strange males.
- **The Old World monkeys** of Africa and Asia rest by sitting down, and have tough pads on their bottoms to prevent sores developing.
- **Some colobus monkeys** gnaw on the charcoal of burned trees to help neutralize the toxins in some leaves.

▼ *Old World monkeys forage for plant food during the day, and rest by night.*

▲ *Colobus monkeys are one of the larger species of Old World monkey.*

● **Red colobus monkeys** often travel in mixed groups with diana monkeys, as the diana monkeys are better at spotting the chimps that prey on colobus monkeys.

● **Talapoin monkeys** in Central Africa live in forests that are frequently flooded. Excellent swimmers, they often sleep on branches overhanging the water.

● **In Japan**, in areas where humans regularly feed macaques, the birth-rate of the animals rockets, leading to groups of up to 1000.

● **The Hanuman grey langur** of India is protected by religious law, in honour of Hanuman, the monkey god.

● **Some Japanese macaques** have learned to dip food in the sea to clean and salt it, and have become good swimmers in the process.

... **FASCINATING FACT** ...
The Barbary macaque is the only primate, apart from humans, living in Europe.

165

Chimpanzees

▲ *Chimpanzees have a repertoire of up to 30 distinct noises for communicating with other members of their social group.*

● **Chimps have a strict social ladder**, with dominant males at the top. These top males recognize property rights, and never steal food from their inferiors.

● **Observers** have noted chimpanzees carefully lifting a fellow chimp's eyelid to remove a speck of grit.

● **Chimps are the best tool-users** after humans. They use grass stems to fish for termites in their mounds, stones and anvils to crack nuts, and chewed leaves as sponges for gathering water.

● **Chimpanzees** actively hunt for meat, especially when plant food is scarce, and collaborate to catch colobus monkeys, young baboons, birds and rodents.

● **If a chimpanzee** finds a tree laden with fruit, it drums on a tree trunk and makes loud panting cries to summon other chimps from many kilometres away for a share of the feast.

● **Bands of male chimpanzees** have been observed attacking and killing all the males in a neighbouring band. Up to a third of adult male chimp deaths result from territorial disputes.

● **Bonobos**, or pygmy chimpanzees, are found in the dense forests along the Congo River. They are darker than other chimps, with longer legs and smaller heads, and walk upright more often.

- **A bonobo named Kanzi**, a very successful participant in language experiments, also learned how to light a barbecue and cook his own sausages.

- **Chimps eat** a range of plants as medicines, to get rid of conditions such as stomach aches and parasitic worms.

◀ *Grooming is a very important activity amongst chimps. It helps to create strong bonds between individuals, and to establish the group's pecking order.*

...FASCINATING FACT...
Chimpanzees reach puberty at about 10 years, give birth every 4 or 5 years, and may live into their 50s.

New World monkeys

◄ Bald uakaris have a variey of area-specific fur colours but the face always ranges from pink to deep red.

● **The howler monkey** has a special throat bone that enables it to produce its distinctive deep roar.

● **The pygmy marmoset** of the upper Amazon Basin is the world's smallest monkey, weighing 125 g.

● **Unlike Old World monkeys**, most New World monkeys have prehensile tails, and can suspend their whole bodies from them when travelling or feeding.

● **New World monkeys** have broad noses with sideways-pointing nostrils; Old World monkeys' noses are narrow, with downward-pointing nostrils.

● **The pygmy marmoset** uses its teeth to gouge holes in tree bark so that it can extract the gum – a major part of its diet.

● **The South American night monkey** is the only truly nocturnal monkey.

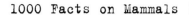
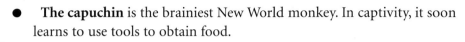

- **The capuchin** is the brainiest New World monkey. In captivity, it soon learns to use tools to obtain food.

- **Marmosets and tamarins** always give birth to twins, carried mainly by the father.

- **Titi monkeys** live in small family groups, and all sleep together with their tails entwined.

◀ *Howler monkeys make ear-shattering calls to warn off rivals.*

> ...FASCINATING FACT...
> Spider monkeys hang by their tails from
> low branches over rivers to drink.

169

Gibbons

- **The gibbons of Southeast Asia** are the smallest and most agile of the apes. They pair for life, and each couple has its own song of whoops and wails.

- **Swinging by their long arms**, gibbons hurtle through the forest, flying up to 15 m between hand-holds.

- **With the longest arms**, relative to body size, of all the primates, gibbons often hang by just one arm.

- **No-one** has been able to keep up with gibbons to time how fast they swing arm over arm (brachiation).

- **Siamangs** are the largest gibbons, at up to 15 kg.

- **About 2 million years ago** there was only one gibbon species, but Ice Age changes in sea levels created forest islands, where separate species developed.

- **A gibbon sleeps** sitting up on a branch with its head between its bent knees, not in a nest like great apes.

- **Gibbons** are more closely related to orang-utans than to the chimps and gorillas of Africa.

- **Gibbons have extremely flexible** shoulder joints, and can rotate through 360° while hanging from one arm.

▲ *Lar gibbons often produce loud calls known as 'duets' in order to reinforce pair-bond relationship between male and female.*

◄ *From earliest infancy, the gibbon spends nearly all its life above ground in the trees.*

> ···**FASCINATING FACT**···
> In the black gibbon species, the male is all black, the female light cream with a black face.

171

Baboons

- **Baboons' feet** are more suited to walking than grabbing branches.

- **Some East African baboons** cooperate in hunting and killing small antelopes, but are unwilling to share the catch.

- **Male Hamadryas baboons** herd their females all the time to keep them from other males.

- **The olive baboons** of the East African highlands live in troops of up to 140 individuals.

- **When old male Hamadryas baboons** are defeated by younger males, they lose weight, and their distinctive grey mantle changes to the colour of the females' hair.

◄ *Olive baboons are group dwellers, but male young are driven off to join other troops when they reach maturity.*

▶ *The male mandrill has a bright blue and red face for attracting females.*

- **Chacma baboons**, found in the far south of Africa, often enter water to feed on water plants or shellfish.

- **For their first few weeks**, baby baboons hang upside down from their mother's chest, but by 4 or 5 months they are riding on her back, like jockeys.

- **The ancient Egyptians** sometimes trained Hamadryas baboons to harvest figs.

- **Baboons** in South Africa's Kruger National Park will risk electric fence shocks to steal food from tourists.

...**FASCINATING FACT**...
Olive baboon males fighting over females will enlist the help of a third male.

What are mammals?

- **Humans** feel close to mammals because they, too, are mammals, with hairy bodies, a large brain and special mammary glands for feeding their young with milk.

- **There are about 4500 species** of mammals in the world (and at least 1 million insect species!).

- **All mammals** except the duckbilled platytpus and spiny anteater give birth to live young.

- **Mammals** evolved from reptiles, but are warm blooded.

- **The two main mammal groups** are the marsupials (whose young develop in the mother's pouch) and placentals.

- **All mammals have three little bones** in their ears that transfer sound vibrations to the inner ear from the eardrum.

- **Mammals** have a variety of teeth

▲ *Some mammals are very vulnerable because of human influences such as hunting or loss of habitat. The tiger is in the 'critically endangered' category on the Red List of Threatened Species.*

shapes: chisels for gnawing, long fangs for fighting and killing prey, sharp-edged slicers and flat-topped crushers.

● **The platypus and spiny anteater** are egg-laying mammals called monotremes.

● **Mammals have a palate** that enables them to breathe through their noses while chewing.

● **Mammals** give a level of maternal care beyond that of other animals.

▼ *Young mammals mature more slowly than other animal young, so they are looked after for longer.*

The first mammals

- **Before true mammals emerged**, some reptiles, such as the dog-like Cynodonts, had developed mammalian characteristics such as hair and specialized teeth.

- **The mammary glands** with which mammals suckle their young evolved from sweat glands – some mammal-like reptiles may have exuded a sort of milk from sweat glands for their young.

- **The earliest true mammals** appeared more than 210 million years ago and were only 15 cm long.

- **One of the best-known** of the earliest fossil mammals was an insect-eater named *Megazostrodon*. The size of a modern shrew, it hunted insects at night.

▼ *The* Uintatherium *was about the size of a hippopotamus and was one of the first large mammals living about 50 million years ago.*

- **A major difference** between mammals and reptiles was the development of the little bones linking the eardrum and inner ear, found only in mammals.

- **In the age of the dinosaurs**, which lasted some 160 million years, mammals stayed very small.

- **All known mammal fossils** from 210 to 66 million years ago would fit into a normal-sized bucket!

- **By the time the dinosaurs became extinct** about 65 million years ago, marsupials, placentals and monotremes had all evolved.

- **Fossils** of very early mammals came from Europe, South Africa and China.

▶ *The tiny* Megazostrodon *kept well hidden from predatory reptiles, and was active at night.*

...FASCINATING FACT...
Within 10 million years of the extinction of the dinosaurs, most modern mammal orders, including horses and primates, had appeared.

Desert life

- **The American kangaroo rat** may never take a drink of water in its life! It derives moisture from its food and by recycling its breath.

- **Prairie dogs** have air-conditioned homes – the air in their tunnels is renewed every 10 minutes by the suction effect of the entrances being at different heights.

- **Desert ground squirrels** have hair on the pads of their feet to insulate them from burning hot sand.

▼ *These dromedary camels are exceptionally well adapted for desert life*

- **Desert bighorn sheep** can let their daytime temperatures rise from 36.8°C to 40°C, re-radiating the excess heat at night.

- **Some desert-dwelling badgers** and sheep have a fatty layer that insulates their internal organs from external heat.

- **The Australian fat-tailed mouse** has a carrot-shaped tail that stores fat, which it lives off during droughts.

- **Most desert mammals** rest in shade or burrows by day, emerging to seek food in the cool of night.

- **Collared peccaries**, or javelinas, are American desert pigs. In times of drought they eat cacti, spines and all.

▲ *On dry plains, prairie dogs may inhabit extensive tunnel-and-nest 'towns' that cover up to 65 hectares.*

- **Desert kit foxes** have hypersensitive hearing – far more useful than a good sense of smell in the dry air.

- **The long legs of the Arabian camel** raise its body to a height where air temperatures are up to 25°C cooler than ground temperatures.

What are rodents?

▲ *Guinea pigs are sociable, tail-less rodents native to South America.*

- **Rodents**, which include mice, squirrels, beavers, porcupines and guinea pigs, have two incisor teeth in each jaw that never stop growing.

- **If a rodent's teeth** are not constantly worn down by gnawing, they can curve round into the animal's skull and kill it – the name 'rodent' means 'gnawer'.

- **Some 40% of all mammal species are rodents**. They range in size from the 1.4-m long capybara to the Baluchistan pygmy jerboa, at 4.7 cm (body length).

- **The earliest-known rodents** appeared in 57-million-year-old fossil beds in both Asia and North America.

- **Two rodents**, the house mouse and the brown rat, occur more widely than any other mammal, and are found on all continents, including Antarctica.

- **Guinea pigs in South America** and edible dormice in Europe have both been bred to be eaten by humans.

- **Female Norway lemmings** can begin to breed when only 14 days old.

- **The fastest rodents** over the ground may be kangaroo mice and jerboas, which can bound along on their hind legs at speeds of up to 48 km/h.

- **In the Miocene period** (23 – 5 million years ago), some South American rodents were the size of rhinos!

- **A female house mouse** can produce 14 litters a year.

▲ *The chipmunk is a squirrel-like rodent found in North America. It lives alone in woodland where it hibernates during the winter months.*

181

Mammals' senses

- **Cheetahs have a band of light-sensitive nerve cells** across their retinas that give clear vision ahead and to the sides.

- **Desert mammals** such as the long-eared kit fox find sharp hearing more useful than a keen sense of smell in the dry air.

- **Polar bears** can smell seals up to 60 km away across the ice.

- **Cats have glands** between their toes that leave an identifying scent when they scratch trees.

- **Blue whales** and fin whales communicate by means of the loudest sounds produced by any living creature (up to 188 dB).

◄ *Large cats have eyes on the front of their heads rather than at the sides, helping them to focus on their prey as they hunt.*

▲ *Whales and dolphins communicate with each other using echolocation.*

● **Baby wood-mice** emit ultrasonic distress calls in their first 10 days to summon their mother.

● **Many nocturnal mammals** have reflective areas in their eyes that help night vision.

● **Migrating whales** can sense the Earth's magnetic field, due to particles of the mineral magnetite in their bodies.

● **The exceptionally large ears** of fennec foxes can detect the sound of termites chewing beneath the ground.

● **Skunks** use a powerful scent weapon to deter their enemies.

Hibernation and dormancy

- **The hibernating dormouse** does not attract the attention of predators because its body temperature is so low that it gives off no body odour.

- **The core body temperature** of some hibernating bats falls below freezing – in some cases as low as -5°C – without harming them.

- **Bears** are not true hibernators, but have a moderately reduced body temperature during their winter sleep, offset by the huge amounts of food that they eat before going to sleep.

- **The raccoon dog** is the only member of the dog family to hibernate.

- **The Eastern European dormouse** and the Canadian woodchuck may spend as much as 9 months of the year in hibernation.

- **Hibernators such as ground squirrels** have internal clocks that cause them to go into hibernation at the usual time of year, even if they are kept in warm conditions with plenty of food.

- **A hibernating bat's breathing rate** falls from about 200 breaths per minute to between 25 and 30 a minute for 3 minutes, followed by an 8 minute no-breathing break.

- **Alaskan ground squirrels**, born at the end of June, start to dig burrows 22 days later, and feed, fatten up and begin to hibernate by the end of August.

- **Brown fat**, found in high levels in hibernating mammals, creates heat as the temperature falls.

> ...FASCINATING FACT...
> Hibernating mammals wake up by shivering violently, creating heat that passes to the brain, the vital organs and the rest of the body.

▼ *Only a few animal species are true hibernators. The dormouse may hibernate for up to nine months, and hedgehogs also sleep through the winter months. Grey squirrels and badgers, however, are not true hibernators.*

Bats

Grey squirrel

Dormouse

Badgers

Hedgehog

Migration

- **Florida manatees** usually migrate south in winter, but recently they have moved instead into the warm water outlets of hydroelectric generating plants.

- **Hooded seals** usually migrate south from Greenland in the Atlantic Ocean, but in 1990 one seal ended up off California in the Pacific, having taken a wrong turn.

- **Migrating noctule bats** established themselves in Hawaii, after being blown 3000 km off course.

- **Migrating whales** travel huge distances with the aid of internal magnetic navigation.

▼ *Reindeer and caribou (North American reindeer) may make short, daily journeys to find food or longer, seasonal migrations of up to 1200 km.*

◀ *It is thought that the blue whale migrates to warmer climates for the winter, when the female will give birth.*

- **Oil pipe-lines** are serious obstacles to caribou, which follow traditional migratory routes every year.

- **Migrating European noctule bats** fly at high altitude, emitting loud, low-frequency sounds at one second intervals to keep in ground contact.

- **American grey squirrels** sometimes travel in their thousands, crossing roads, rivers and towns in their search for food.

- **Beluga whales** return to the estuaries where they were born to give birth.

- **Over 1 million wildebeest** take part in a circular seasonal migration in east Africa's Serengeti region.

...FASCINATING FACT...
Each year, grey whales migrate
20,000 km in all, going to and from their
breeding grounds.

Arctic life

- **White fur** helps creatures such as Arctic hares to hide from predators in the snow, but also helps predators such as polar bears avoid detection as they hunt.

- **The ringed seal**, the most northerly of the seals, has been reported at the North Pole itself.

- **Polar bears** and Arctic foxes have tiny ears to reduce the loss of body heat in the icy Arctic.

▲ *The Arctic fox has incredibly thick fur to keep out the cold. It also has very small ears, and short legs and tail to prevent heat loss.*

- **Narwhals** and belugas migrate from the Arctic to warm estuaries and fjords to give birth, returning to the pack ice in late summer.

- **The bulky Arctic musk ox** has a double coat of dense wool overlaid with thick hair, and can stay in the Arctic all year, surviving temperatures of -70°C.

- **During blizzards**, musk oxen form a circle with the calves protected in the centre from the wind and snow.

- **The walrus** is a permanent inhabitant of the Arctic region, spending much of its life on the pack ice.

- **The ringed seal** gives birth in a snow cave, entered from the water through a hole in the ice.

- **Inuit hunters** fear a female walrus defending her calf more than they fear a polar bear.

- **In winter and spring**, Arctic foxes depend on scavenging from polar bear seal-kills – but can end up on the menu themselves!

◄ *In the past, the musk ox has been hunted to near extinction by humans. Fortunately, there are now conservation programmes which are regenerating the population.*

189

What are marsupials?

▲ *The American or virginia opossum is nocturnal and a good climber and swimmer.*

- **Marsupials** are born in a tiny, undeveloped form, and many spend months in a protective pouch, attached to a teat.

- **Marsupials** probably originated in America some 100 million years ago, at a time when America and Australia were still joined.

- **The red kangaroo** is the largest living marsupial today.

- **Marsupial mouse**, marsupial rat and marsupial mole are the popular names of some Australian marsupials, but they are not in fact related to mice, rats or moles.

- **Marsupials have slightly lower body temperatures** than most other mammals, and have smaller brains than placentals of a similar size.

- **Two thirds of all marsupials** live in Australia and New Guinea; one third are mainly South American opossums.

- **The only aquatic marsupial** is a South American opossum.

- **The wombat's pouch** faces backwards, so that the young are protected from pieces of flying earth when the mother is digging.

- **In Australia**, kangaroos fill the plains-grazing niche occupied elsewhere by antelopes and gazelles (placental mammals).

- **Many small marsupials**, including some opossums, do not have pouches.

▼ *Native to Australia, the red kangaroo is the largest of the marsupials and lives in groups on dry, open grassland.*

Communication

- **Whales' low frequency calls** travel thousands of km through the water.

- **Some whales communicate** with complex 'songs'. All the individuals in one ocean region sing the same song.

- **Some of the puppies** from the litter of a poodle bred with a jackal had the poodle's 'language'; others had the jackal's. But the two groups could not communicate with one another.

- **Male chimps** establish their status by seeing who can make the most noise.

- **One chimp learned** to use 130 gestures of American Sign Language.

- **Cats and dogs** erect the hair on parts of their bodies to impress rivals and mates, or frighten off predators.

- **Cats mark their territories** by scratching tree trunks, imparting their scents from glands between their toes.

- **A well-fed lion** can walk head-up through a herd of antelope without panicking them, but if its head is low, the antelope run, knowing it is hunting.

- **The sifaka lemur** has one alarm call to warn of birds of prey, and another to warn of snakes.

- **Many young mammals** have a 'play' body language just for mock fights.

◄ *Members of the dog family use ear positions as part of their language.*

► *Chimps communicate using a wide range of facial expressions.*

Parental care in mammals

- **Many mammals carry their young** around with them. Some bats even go hunting with a youngster aboard.

- **Mother whales** have to nudge and encourage newly born young up to the surface to take their first breath, often aided by 'aunts' from the same pod.

- **In wild dog packs**, several females may take turns to suckle and guard all the young in the group.

- **Sperm whale** offspring may suckle for up to 15 years.

- **Elephant young** are born after 22 months. Several of the herd cows help the new baby to stand.

- **Mother cheetahs** teach their young how to hunt by bringing small live prey back for them to practice on.

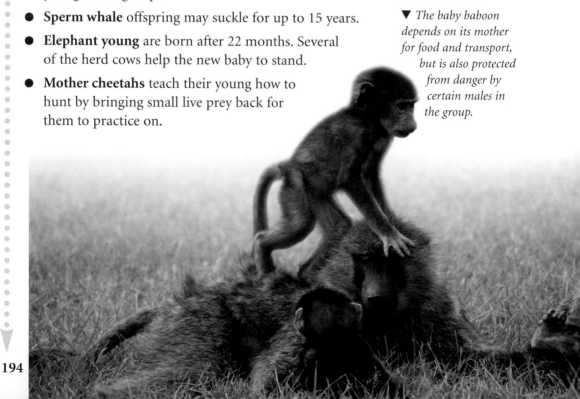

▼ *The baby baboon depends on its mother for food and transport, but is also protected from danger by certain males in the group.*

194

▲ *Elephants live in family groups of females and their young, led by a dominant female.*

- **A big cat female** carries her young by holding the entire head in her mouth, in a gap behind her teeth.

- **Young kangaroos** leave the pouch at 5–11 months, but continue to stick their head in to suckle for 6 months.

- **Many cats**, large and small, start to train their young by allowing them to attack their twitching tails.

... FASCINATING FACT ...
Baby gorillas may only climb on the silver-back while they still have a white rump tuft.

195

Ice Age mammals

- **Woolly mammoths** adapted to Ice Age conditions by developing a thick coat of dark hair, and using their enormous tusks to sweep snow off the grasses they ate.

- **The woolly rhinoceros** was up to 5 m long, and roamed the tundras of northern Europe and Asia. Like the mammoth, it featured in the cave drawings of hunters.

- **Several Ice Age mammals** became giant-sized to help them combat the cold, including aurochs – the giant ancestors of modern cattle.

- **Many mammoths** are so well preserved in the Siberian permafrost that their flesh is still edible, and their last meals remain in their stomachs.

- **On the tundra** at the edge of the ice sheets, some mammals migrated south in winter; others, like the huge European cave bear, hibernated in their lairs.

- ***Smilodon***, a large sabre-toothed cat, inhabited Ice Age North America, dying out along with many of the large animals it preyed on.

- **Many mammal species** died out between 12,000 and 10,000 years ago, as the last Ice Age ended. But some survived, including musk-oxen, horses, hyenas and saiga antelopes.

- **The Ice Age bison** were similar to modern bison, but had sweeping 1-m long horns on either side of their heads.

- **The giant short-faced bear**, which inhabited North America until the end of the last Ice Age, was twice the size of the Kodiak bear, had long legs and weighed up to 1 tonne.

▶ *The woolly mammoth had small ears to prevent heat-loss, and beneath its hairy skin was a thick layer of heat-preserving fat.*

◀ *Sabre-toothed* Smilodon *ranged from Canada to Argentina. It used its huge upper canine teeth to slice through the tough hides of large prey animals and bite out big chunks of flesh.*

...FASCINATING FACT...
Cave bears used the same caves for many generations. One cave in Austria contained the bones of up to 50,000 individual bears.

Camouflage

- **Stripes** benefit both predators and prey by breaking up the body shape, for example in tigers and zebras.

- **The simplest camouflage** makes an animal a similar colour to its surroundings, such as the white of a polar bear in snow.

- **Some whales** and dolphins are dark on top and light underneath, camouflaging them against the dark of deep water or the light of the sky.

- **Some camouflage** mimics the broken shapes of light shining through trees, as in the dappled markings of giraffes.

▶ *The pattern of a giraffe's coat (which remains the same all through life) varies according to area and is an important camouflage tool.*

- **The young of many mammal species**, such as lions and pigs, have early camouflage markings that disappear as the animals grow older.

- **The coats of Arctic foxes** and hares change from dark in summer to white in winter.

- **Bold markings**, such as the contrasting shapes of the oryx, camouflage by breaking up body outline.

- **The bobcat's spots** camouflage it in rocks, while the similar-shaped plain lynx merges with forest.

- **The elephant's huge grey form** disappears as it stands still in the shadows.

▲ *The orca's light underparts make it less visible against the water's surface in daytime.*

> **...FASCINATING FACT...**
> Not all camouflage is visual –
> some mammals roll in dung to disguise
> their own scents.

New World marsupials

- **American marsupials** are nearly all from the opossum family, which has lived in America for 55 million years.

- **Opossums** have spread successfully northwards as far as Canada, but are vulnerable to frostbitten ears and tails.

- **When attacked**, the opossum goes into a death-like trance, called 'playing 'possum'.

- **Opossums entwine** their prehensile tails around those of their young when carrying them.

- **The Virginia opossum** usually has 13 teats in its pouch, but often gives birth to a higher number of young. Those that are not able to attach to a teat soon die.

- **The yapok**, or water opossum, is the only mainly aquatic marsupial. It has webbed rear feet.

- **The monito del monte** is a rat-sized marsupial unrelated to opossums, and found in Chile's cool forests.

- **Once a baby opossum has attached itself** to a teat, it cannot let go until it is fully developed.

- **The newly born mouse opossum** is no larger than a grain of rice – the smallest new-born mammal.

▶ *Opossums generally only group together at breeding time.*

...FASCINATING FACT...
The Maya civilization of Central America
believed the opossum to be a magical
animal.

The mating game

- **In some species** of Australian marsupial mouse, the male dies after a two-week mating period.

- **A beaver stays with its mate** for many years, producing a new litter each year.

- **A male hedgehog** courts a female by circling her, sometimes wearing a deep groove in the soil, until she accepts him.

- **Male Californian sea-lions** bark to guard their mating territory. Underwater, the barks produce bursts of bubbles.

- **The hooded seal** impresses females by inflating a nostril lining into a red balloon.

▲ *The mandrill's facial markings and reddish-blue rump signify to females his suitability as a mate.*

- **The red markings** on a male mandrill's blue and red face become brighter during the mating season.

- **To attract potential mates**, orang-utan males emit a series of loud roars that tail off into groans.

- **White rhino males** have strict territorial boundaries. They try to keep receptive females within the territory, but if a female strays outside, he will not follow her.

- **Hippos** prefer to mate in the water, with the female often completely submerged, and having to raise her head to breathe every so often.

▼ *A male narwhal's tusk can be up to 3 m long, and is actually one of its only two teeth.*

...**FASCINATING FACT**...
Narwhal males compete for mates by 'fencing' with their long, spiral tusks.

Life on the plains

- **In the 1800s**, a vast springbok herd, 25 km wide and 160 km long, crossed the plains of southern Africa.

- **The Argentine maned wolf** has extremely long legs for hunting in the tall pampas grasses.

- **The African springhare** resembles a miniature kangaroo. It grazes at night on floodplains.

- **The world's biggest grouping of large land mammals** takes place every year on Africa's Serengeti plains, with the migration of 1.5 million wildebeest and 1 million other hoofed animals.

- **Savannah buffalo** graze on tall, coarse grasses, reducing them to the height preferred by other grazers.

- **New-born wildebeest** have a strong instinct to approach anything that moves – even, fatally, hyenas or lions.

◀ *The pronghorn communicates over long distances.*

▲ *Wildebeest are herd animals, although males form their own separate groups.*

- **As herds of wildebeest** trample and manure the ground, they stimulate the rapid regrowth of grasses.

- **If young wild dogs tire** while hunting on Africa's Okavango flood plain, the adults hide them and return for them later.

- **The American pronghorn antelope** can see the white warning patches on the rump of another pronghorn from several kilometres away.

- **The Bactrian camel** of Central Asia eats salty plants avoided by other grazers.

205

Heat regulation

◄ *The coat of a bighorn sheep comprises a double layer of hairs to protect it from harsh winds and snow.*

- **Fruit bats** are susceptible to heat stroke, so to keep themselves cool, some lick themselves all over and fan cool air at their bodies with their wings.

- **The oryx** has special blood vessels in its nose to keep its blood temperature low in the desert heat.

- **Large-eared desert species** such as fennec foxes use their ears as radiators to get rid of body heat.

- **The desert bighorn sheep** draws air over a thickly veined area of its throat to cool its blood.

- **Wallowing in mud** keeps pigs cool and protects their skin from the sun.

- **A hippos' skin** exudes a red, lacquer-like substance to protect it from sunburn.

- **During hot spells**, kangaroos lick their wrists a lot, so that the evaporation of the saliva causes cooling.

- **Indian zebu cattle** have more sweat glands than western cattle, and maintain a lower body temperature, making them common in China, Africa and South America.

- **The eland's temperature** can rise several degrees without causing sweating, allowing it to conserve 5 litres of water daily.

- **After feeding their young**, mother bats often leave them in the heat of the cave and perch near the cooler entrance.

▼ *Hippopotamuses spend much of their time submerged in water as their skin quickly dries out and cracks in the hot African sun.*

207

Index

Index

Index

Index

Index

216

Index

Index

Index

Acknowledgements

The publishers would like to thank the following artists who
have contributed to this book:

Jim Channell, Wayne Ford, Chris Forsey, LR Galante
(Galante Studio), Ian Jackson, Emma Louise Jones,
Steve Kirk, Kevin Maddision, Alan Male (Linden Artists),
Steve Roberts, Eric Robson (Illustration), Mike Saunders,
Sarah Smith (Linden Artists)

All pictures from the Miles Kelly Archives, Corbis
Professional Collections, Corel Corporation, Photodisc